Digital HR

A Guide to Technology-Enabled Human Resources

T0350604

DIGITAL HR

A Guide to Technology-Enabled Human Resources

Deborah Waddill

Society for Human Resource Management
Alexandria, Virginia | shrm.org

Society for Human Resource Management, India Office
Mumbai, India | shrmindia.org

Society for Human Resource Management
Haidian District Beijing, China | shrm.org/cn

Society for Human Resource Management, Middle East and Africa Office
Dubai, UAE | shrm.org/pages/mena.aspx

SOCIETY FOR HUMAN
RESOURCE MANAGEMENT

The Society for Human Resource Management is the world's largest HR professional society, representing 285,000 members in more than 165 countries. For nearly seven decades, the society has been the leading provider of resources serving the needs of HR professionals and advancing the practice of human resource management. SHRM has more than 575 affiliated chapters within the United States and subsidiary offices in China, India, and United Arab Emirates. Please visit us at www.shrm.org.

Library of Congress Cataloging-in-Publication Data has been applied for and is on file with the Library of Congress. ISBN (pbk): 978-1-586-44542-3; ISBN (PDF): 978-1-586-44543-0; ISBN (EPUB): 978-1-586-44544-7; ISBN (MOBI): 978-1-586-44545-4

Printed in the United States of America

FIRST EDITION

PB Printing   10 9 8 7 6 5 4 3 2 1   61.14521 | 18-0266

Table of Contents

PART II
LEARNING MANAGEMENT

PART III
TALENT MANAGEMENT

PART IV
KNOWLEDGE MANAGEMENT

Foreword

Over the last half-century, human resources (HR) has become ever more critical to the success, if not survival, of all organizations. The emergence of new technologies and tools has placed HR professionals in the center of business strategy and operations. Executives increasingly rely on HR to mold company culture and performance through strategic planning, change management, and effective technology implementation. This growing importance of HR has modified the role of HR professionals; they must now serve as critical business partners who fashion strategy and lead change, while continuing to serve as employee champions.

As a thought leader in the area of HR technologies, Dr. Deborah Waddill offers insight regarding the ways in which HR leaders can best select, govern, implement, and assess HR technologies while harnessing the power of these new trends. In this text, *Digital HR*, Dr. Waddill addresses the ascendance of HR and explains how the major "disruptive" trends are reshaping HR. The emergent trends include (a) cloud computing, (b) social media, (c) big data and analytics, (d) mobile technology, and (e) the Internet of Things.

An overriding theme of the book is Dr. Waddill's emphasis on the necessity for HR to engage in strategic thinking and planning, which enables better management in every phase of organizational life, be it staffing, marketing, operations, or training. Throughout the pages of this book, Dr. Deborah Waddill identifies the important issues and highlights the critical questions that help readers consider and develop a unique HR technology strategy for their own organizations. Case studies demonstrate how HR departments in world-class organizations such as IBM, Panasonic, Cornerstone OnDemand, and others leverage technology to maximize employee engagement and improve performance. Examples like these prove that well-developed and well-applied HR technologies can enhance the business value of the HR department and overall organizational success.

One of the many great features in this book is the emphasis on the Shared Service Center (SSC) Model approach as a platform for integrating HR throughout the organization. Dr. Waddill deftly establishes a connection between optimal organizational performance, the SSC model, and implementation of a Human Resource Information System. The SSC serves as a hub of HR functions and information; this model requires that HR professionals have access to reliable data, available through an HR system. Along with a justification for the SSC model and the need for an HR system, readers will find in these chapters a solid guide for selection and implementation of a wide variety of technologies that can be used as standalone features or in conjunction with others to maximize HR efficiency and effectiveness.

HR technologies can dramatically improve every aspect of organizational life and create multiple opportunities for success. Dr. Deborah Waddill is a leading thinker regarding the relationship between technology and HR, having been a consultant, researcher, teacher, and global speaker on all aspects of HR, leadership, and HR technologies. This book will surely become the top handbook for anyone who wishes to understand the complexity and tap the power of technology for the HR profession. In these pages, Dr. Waddill skillfully guides the reader to implement carefully crafted HR technology strategies for a lasting, positive impact on organizational growth and effectiveness.

—Dr. Michael J. Marquardt
Professor of Human Resource Development
and International Affairs,
The George Washington University
President, World Institute for Action Learning

Preface

PURPOSE OF AND USES FOR THIS BOOK

Welcome to the world of technology-enabled human resources (digital HR). You are embarking on the journey toward understanding the technologies important to HR functions. This text will inform you about key HR technology terms and related topics. It is not its intention to address every new technology; rather, the text examines technology types and groupings to offer an overview of how they can positively impact HR. The goal is for you to understand the valuable contributions you can make in the planning, selection, design, implementation, and evaluation of technology without being a technology expert. The technologies discussed in this book impact anyone with people-development or people-management responsibilities. Each chapter addresses the "disruptive technologies," as they are called, and how they can be harnessed to benefit an organization's HR practice. Legal and regulatory issues are also addressed. In the introduction to the chapter you will find an overview of the technologies in that chapter and their general relevance to HR and the HR technology strategy. In short, it is an explanation of why you should care about the contents of the chapter. Located at the end of each chapter are some resources for digging deeper if you want to examine a given topic in more depth. And each chapter uses questions to encourage you to consider how the topic relates to your organization's overarching HR technology strategy.

Those who have direct people care or other HR responsibilities and who are unfamiliar with the full range of technologies available to HR professionals will benefit from this book. Readers may include business owners, executives, managers, and information technology (IT) and HR professionals.

Since the technology strategy of your organization is of utmost importance when making a technology decision, the first chapter describes the components of an HR technology strategy. The HR technology strategy theme is carried throughout the entire text. As you are reading through the text, consider where your organization is today on the HR technology spectrum (the "as is" or current mode of operation [CMO]), then consider the technologies and case studies presented and begin to cast a vision of the future (the "to be" or future mode of operation [FMO]). How would that vision benefit HR constituents and stakeholders?

Explore and analyze the HR technology strategy in order to mature the future mode of operation. Ask questions. The HR technology strategy must be directed by HR professionals with HR expertise. Knowledge of technology is needed but you do not need to be a technology expert to direct the vision.

Technology terms are italicized and defined at first use. "Tips and Tools" boxes include recommendations and trial versions of the technology when available. End-of-chapter questions prod reflection on how the technology could align with or extend your organization's HR technology strategy. The "Digging Deeper" sections offer you lists of current resources for research beyond the text.

You will not see many vendor names, since each geographical region offers a variety of vendors too numerous to list. As an alternative, we suggest that you join a local or regional HR association or community of practice (such as those on LinkedIn or the Society for Human Resource Management's [SHRM] website) to identify a list of reliable vendors, consultants, subcontractors, and so on available where you work. Remember, it is very important to find a regional HR association or community of practice (CoP) in which you can participate. These groups will benefit you both intellectually and professionally. Further, your connections may provide much-needed support for your technology-related decisions.

I hope you will turn to this guide again and again as you participate in and contribute to technology decisions in your workplace! Enjoy!

PART I

TECHNOLOGY-ENABLED HUMAN RESOURCES

CHAPTER 1

Technology and Its Impact on Human Resources and Business Professionals

TOPICS COVERED IN THIS CHAPTER

- HR technology terminology

- Impact of HR technology on HR roles

- HR competencies and technology

- Gauging organizational readiness for HR technology

- The competitive edge—effective HR strategy

- HR strategy and leadership

It is an exciting time to be in the human resources field. We are seeing the impact of the technology revolution, now labeled by some as the "Digital Age" or the "Fourth Industrial Revolution." This is no small transformation. All of the major consulting firms offer the same prognosis. Forrester, Gartner, McKinsey, Deloitte, and others point to the radical alteration the disruptive technologies, such as social media, cloud computing, data analytics, and mobile, have on the way we do business. They also have impacted HR.

In fact, HR has perhaps been most shaken up by this technology revolution. As one part of the organization that connects with all workers at every employment stage from recruitment to separation, HR now has systems available in the form of HR information systems, human capital management systems, and HR management systems that handle the entire employee life cycle and more. The new HR systems provide predictive analytics and management services never seen before in technology.

Here is the twist: Perhaps for the first time, HR is in the driver's seat, fully entrenched in the executive suite making critical decisions that impact the organization. "Digital HR" is the new professional nomenclature for those HR departments that embrace these new technologies.

Empowered by technology, HR is evolving toward[1]

- Modern, dynamic, and networked organizations that thrive on organizational structure based on small, agile work teams;
- Ongoing employee learning, enabling a learning environment that is flexible and on demand;
- Acquisition of talent using leading-edge technology;
- Enhanced employee engagement that thrives on technologies such as social networking, prescriptive analytics, and cloud-enabled access to resources;
- Performance appraisal models that offer continuous (not periodic) feedback; and
- An HR experience that thrives on mobile applications, artificial intelligence (AI), and other innovations.

In a *Workforce* article entitled "HR 2018 Future View," a panel of futurists forecasted (1) the rise of virtual teams enabled by videoconferencing; (2) recruitment using virtual, global, and just-in-time tools tied to a return-on-investment (ROI); (3) data-driven decision–making; (4) continuous learning supported by technology; and (5) a talent management strategy primarily reliant upon systems.[2] Now, more than a decade later, all of these technology predictions have come true. Even the expected HR competencies and roles have shifted.

HR TECHNOLOGY TERMINOLOGY

There is a whole new genre of systems that handle all of the talent management functions. They are called human capital management (HCM) systems. HCM has emerged in full force, with systems that can handle every aspect of the talent management process. By definition, *human capital management* is "the comprehensive set of practices for recruiting, managing, developing, and optimizing the human resources of an organization."[3]

For some people, the term human capital management is offensive, as it implies that humans are a type of inanimate object. Understanding that the term is simply meant to encompass all processes of talent management, for the purposes of this text "HCM" and "talent management" will be used interchangeably. The terms represent the powerful and all-encompassing talent management systems forecasted above.[4]

IMPACT OF HR TECHNOLOGIES ON HR ROLES

Not surprisingly, the new HR technologies—including HCM—have an impact on HR roles. As technology gains importance, it supports—and in some cases, supplants—many of the people-care functions that HR professionals previously handled themselves. In leading organizations, conventional HR functions have shifted to frontline managers who are tasked with people management, or "people care." In this situation, HR professionals partner with managers who provide the people care, while HR takes on the role of HR business partner (HRBP). An HRBP is an HR professional with a customer service mindset who understands the organization's vision and mission, applies policies that align with the objectives, and executes the HR strategy.

The changes to roles have also impacted the HR generalist and HR specialist positions, making them less prevalent. Organizations now often refer to HR professionals with the following terms:[5]

- Strategic partner (typically an executive role)
- Change agent as HRBP
- Administrative expert (often providing expertise in a shared service center)
- Employee champion as HRBP

Under this new paradigm of roles and responsibilities, HR professionals must develop new competencies to fulfill the roles of strategic partner, change agent, employee champion, and administrative expert.

HR COMPETENCIES AND TECHNOLOGY

With the shift to new roles and the introduction of new, powerful HR technologies, the required set of HR competencies have also changed. Promoted by organizations such as SHRM and the HR Certification Institute (HRCI), HR competencies in the twenty-first century differ from those in the twentieth century primarily because of the need for skills that are technology related. For instance, with the advent of social media, necessary communication skills include an understanding of how to create and share content through media for HR purposes. Critical analysis skills must include an understanding of how to use big data to inform HR decisions.

In 2015, HRCI collected over thirty thousand worldwide surveys rating the competencies and performance of more than four thousand HR professionals in 1,500 organizations. In accordance with this study, SHRM provides a set of nine competencies for the HR professional. Two of the nine are related to technology—communication and critical evaluation.[6]

Technology supports, extends, and enhances all HR functions and, if used properly, can ultimately increase the effectiveness of an HR individual, team, department, and organization. HR professionals must have the skills and competencies to maximize the inherent value of these technologies.

GAUGING ORGANIZATIONAL READINESS FOR HR TECHNOLOGIES

An HR professional, whether executive, manager, strategic planner, change agent, administrative expert, or employee champion, interfaces with the technologies used within an organization. As a growing number of HR-specific technologies emerge, the organization's culture and its disposition toward new technology become increasingly relevant. It is HR's responsibility to assess the organization's readiness for new technologies.

A 2017 *McKinsey* article titled "Culture for a Digital Age" provides insight to the assessment of organizational readiness for new technology. The article identifies culture as one of the main barriers to a company's successful implementation of new technologies. The following are key elements of culture that prohibit an organization from moving forward and embracing new digital-age technologies.[7]

- Functional and departmental silos,
- Fear of taking risks, and
- A lack of customer-centric mentality.

Overcoming these cultural roadblocks is the job of the HR department. Let's first determine what they are and then how to overcome them.

Functional Silos

Functional silos represent what Goran, LaBerge, and Srinivasan call a "narrow, parochial mentality of workers who hesitate to share information or collaborate across functions."[8] Silos have existed within organizations for decades, but the relevance to this situation is that they prevent an organization from supporting and investing in HR technologies that would benefit employees in all of the business units, not just the HR department. This narrow viewpoint can be overcome using simple methods such as routine management job rotation, multidisciplinary teams, and data transparency and sharing, all of which are best enabled by technology.

Fear of Taking Risks

An organization that is risk averse will lack innovation. Risk-taking must not be reckless and implemented on a large scale; rather, it should be inculcated in the culture by allowing small risks. Giving frontline workers the tools and decision-making ability to handle issues can combat risk-averseness. It also frees up the otherwise rigid approach to decision-making in general.

Lack of Customer-Centric Mentality

The lack of a customer-centric view also restricts the adoption of new technologies. When the customer comes first, management is compelled to provide the tools to properly serve the customer. These should be leading-edge approaches; for example, collecting and analyzing big data available through practices and systems that provide current, ongoing information about the customer interests, preferences, and needs. A customer focus requires investment in the technologies and tools necessary to provide excellent customer service.

Elements like the organization's vision and mission, management philosophy, the tone of labor-management interactions, and the degree of shared agreement about the technology also impact an organization's readiness for a new technology. Is the organization adaptive and receptive to new technologies, or is it more resistant to technology and the changes it will render? Does the organization view technology as fundamental to its success, or are the technologies viewed as peripheral to the organization's goals and therefore of lesser priority?

Why do you care about identifying your organization's predisposition toward technology? Because it will govern how you approach introducing a new technology. This is especially important if the new technology is one that will upset the organizational norms. In that case, you will need to be an employee champion who is also a change agent. Your assessment of the organization's stance toward technology in general then provides an indicator of the level of resistance you can expect toward new HR technologies. Remember that the majority of organizational change efforts fail.[9] Consequently, in order to mitigate potential failure of a new technology, your understanding of the organization's stance toward technology should cause you to adjust your approach. The intensity of your role as change agent will vary based on the receptivity of your organization toward technology.

The more resistant to technology your employees and organization are, the more preliminary work you will have to do.

THE COMPETITIVE EDGE: EFFECTIVE HR STRATEGY

Introducing a new technology is not a simple endeavor. It requires assessment regarding the level of pushback that will be met and an overarching HR technology strategy.

An HR technology strategy is separate from and builds upon the organizational strategy. The organizational strategy drives the competencies and behaviors that employees must have. HR must develop a strategy that includes the HR approach to policies and practices that further the organizational strategy. HR must first formulate and execute policies and practices that produce the employee competencies and behavior to achieve the organization's strategic aims. Second, HR must align the HR technologies with the organizational strategy and in support of the required employee competencies, skills, and behaviors. This is why the HR technology strategy is extremely important: it is both the blueprint and roadmap for the HR technology selection and implementation necessary to support the organizational strategy.

An HR technology strategy that aligns with that of the organization requires the following:[10]

- A mission statement that includes the organization's present purpose;
- A vision statement of the organization's goals for the future;
- Details of HR technology goals and objectives;
- Logistics defining how the HR technology strategy will accomplish its goals and objectives;
- Methods for measuring achievement of HR technology strategy goals and objectives;
- Budget detailing resources and measures needed to implement the strategy;
- Timeline or schedule for completing the objectives, typically three to five years; and
- Yearly reevaluation, assessment, and (if necessary) adjustment of the HR technology strategy.

A graphic representation of this approach can be found in Figure 1.1.

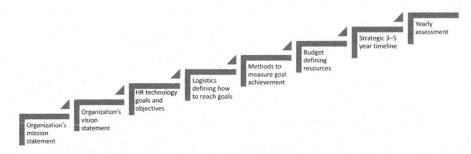

Figure 1.1. HR Technology Strategy Components

HR TECHNOLOGY STRATEGY AND LEADERSHIP

Twenty-first century HR practice requires a bold new leadership approach that is neither top-down nor authoritarian as we saw in the twentieth century. Rather, the HR leader must be authentic, collaborative, transformational, and inspiring. HR must make decisions that will impact the organization's financial well-being. You, as an HR decision-maker, should institute policies that demonstrate your value using best business practices and measurable positive outcomes. You cannot fly under the radar nor can you allow others to make these important decisions for the HR department.

A lack of knowledge about HR technologies should not hobble your leadership. Instead, embrace the leadership role and work in conjunction with your Information Technology department and other business units to find the best solutions. You must collaborate with the business units, employees, and IT professionals in the decision-making and technology selection process.

Leadership of this caliber requires humility and a learning disposition. HR leaders must seek information from the best possible sources using benchmarking, current literature, CoPs, and formal learning opportunities to inform and underpin their decisions. We must inspire others with our vision and demonstrate how the chosen technologies empower employees.

No one should have to clean up after failed HR technology implementations. As HR professionals and leaders, we should have the forethought, organizational knowledge, change agent approach, and skill to avoid such failures. HR professionals are now in the driver's seat. We can implement change proactively by communicating. We need to use the appropriate technologies to develop workers and empower them by giving them the training and tools they need. Throughout this text we will emphasize your role as a leader to design and execute an informed, successful HR technology strategy.

TIPS AND TOOLS FOR HR TECHNOLOGY STRATEGY

- Identify your organization's strategy, then consider how HR can support and advance it.
- Examine the organizational readiness and context for new technologies to gauge change agent role.
- Assess your HR departments' competencies and technologies and their fit with the overall organizational technology strategy.
- Create an HR technology strategy that aligns with the organization's strategy.
- Reassess and adjust the HR technology strategy periodically.

GOING FORWARD

HR professionals must be aware of those technologies that can be used to fulfill the mission and vision of the organization. We must be involved in the technology selection and implementation processes as well as in the business process redesign. We should take advantage of the new, sophisticated, labor-saving hardware and software, and represent employees' best interests in the technology selection process. In so doing we add to our own credibility by being knowledgeable about HR technologies. HR professionals must design an HR technology strategy that reflects the organization's mission and vision while taking into account the organizational readiness for technology.

The present business challenges cannot be solved using solutions from the past. The HR skill sets that were acceptable in the twentieth century will not suffice in the twenty-first; they must be revamped and updated to incorporate new communication and critical analysis tools. Additionally, we cannot and should not let others make important technology decisions for us, foisting upon us solutions that are not custom-designed to solve HR challenges. Instead, HR professionals need to take the lead to design and implement the HR technology strategy.

End-of-Chapter HR Technology Strategy Questions

Considering your organization's overall business strategy, answer the following:

1. What is your organization's HR technology strategy and how does it align with your organization's mission and vision?
2. What additions or modifications to your organization's HR technology strategy would you suggest to ensure its success?

We will refer to your organization's HR technology strategy as a living document, subject to review and revision based upon learnings gleaned about major HR technologies and trends. If your organization has no HR technology strategy, this is your opportunity to influence and guide the development of one.

Digging Deeper

Berger, Lance A., and Dorothy R. Berger. 2018. *The Talent Management Handbook: Making Culture a Competitive Advantage by Acquiring, Identifying, Developing, and Promoting the Best People.* 3rd ed. New York: McGraw Hill.

Decker, Phillip, Roger Durand, Clifton Mayfield, Christy McCormack, David Skinner, and Grady Perdue. 2012. "Predicting Implementation Failure in Organization Change." *Journal of Organizational Culture, Communications and Conflict* 16 (2): 9–49.

Dessler, Gary, and Biju Varkkey. 2016. *Human Resource Management.* 14th ed. Noida, Ind.: Pearson.

Goran, Julie, Laura LaBerge, and Ramesh Srinivasan. 2017. "Culture for a Digital Age." *McKinsey Quarterly,* July 2017, 1–13.

Harvard Business Review. 2011. *HBR's 10 Must Reads on Strategy.* Edited by Harvard Business Review. Boston, MA: Harvard Business Review Press.

CHAPTER 2

Technology Trends in Digital Human Resources

TOPICS COVERED IN THIS CHAPTER

- Five major technology trends
- The intersection between the trends
- Security
- Trends and general technologies
- Cloud computing options
- Internet-of-things applied to HR
- HR's role, new technology trends and the worker
- Regulatory and legal issues regarding technology

The adoption and acceptance of technology depends in part on the characteristics of the organizational culture into which it is introduced, as noted in Chapter 1. Whether an organization is putting into place an entirely new technology system, upgrading an existing system, or implementing a new module in a system, the employees who use the technology must be considered. If workers do not use the technology, it will languish and the investment will be a net loss. This is why so many change efforts fail: the employees are not considered or involved in the initiative.

HR professionals understand the employees, the culture, and the organizational readiness for a new technology. We are, therefore, crucial to the selection, implementation, and adoption of new technology. It is our knowledge of the intended audience and inclusion of stakeholders in technology decisions that will promote its success. Further, HR professionals have the skills and competencies to identify how the technology will impact workflow, jobs, training, benefits, organizational policies, the quality of work life, and so on.

It is satisfying to most HR professionals to assist others. Human resources is, at its very core, dedicated to the development and implementation of employee-related programs that solve business problems. An understanding of and connection with employees—inherent to the HR profession—will provide insights for implementing a new system, process, or program.

When a new technology is introduced, there is a ripple effect through the entire organization. Depending on how well the organization prepares its staff for the change, the ripple may result in manageable waves or it may cause a tsunami of negative reaction. This resistance can take the form of people refusing to participate in the change initiative, vying against or undercutting the changed leadership, altering the scope and direction of the project, spreading unflattering messages about the system, refusing to use the system, and other passive-aggressive behaviors. In the final analysis, a failed change effort is one where the system is not utilized by the intended audience.

In the last chapter, we said that HR functions are impacted by technology. For the purposes of this text, we will group HR functions into three domains: learning management, talent management, and knowledge management. These three domains of HR intersect in the digital realm (see Figure 2.1).

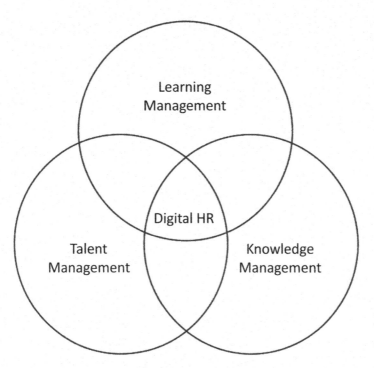

Figure 2.1. HR Domains and Technology

In this chapter we will examine the major trends in technology that—both now and going forward—can be considered to have either a disruptive or liberating influence on these three HR domains. The five significant technology trends that we will address are (1) social media, (2) big data and data analytics, (3) mobile computing, (4) cloud computing, and (5) the Internet of Things (IoT). The impact of these trends on learning management, talent management, and knowledge management domains will be detailed in subsequent chapters. The relevance of these trends for you as an HR professional and the strategy questions about their relationship to HR technology appear in this and subsequent chapters.

FIVE MAJOR TECHNOLOGY TRENDS

The major technology trends have been written about in depth by all of the major consulting firms. HR technology literature categorizes these trends under social media, big data and data analytics, mobility, cloud computing, and IoT. They are often referred to as disruptive technologies because they are changing the HR field in dramatic ways. Organizations that adopt and incorporate these technologies in their HR technology strategy see a profound effect on functions, systems, job descriptions, policies, procedures, and business practices. Adopting these trends requires dramatic adaptations. Additionally, each of these technology groupings must be examined in light of privacy and security when included in the overall HR strategy.

Initiatives to adopt these technologies can impact and improve HR business practices when implemented in the overall technology strategy. They can increase productivity and employee engagement as well as provide exciting new opportunities. For instance, organization-based social media offers HR valuable information about employee interests and concerns while increasing employee engagement. Cloud computing enables mobile access to cloud-enabled tools from anywhere, which can result in increased task efficiencies. Mobility offers just-in-time information at point-of-need using tools that most employees carry with them at all times. HR analytics opens the door to new understandings of employee patterns of behavior, interaction, and technology use by examining the big data collected through a variety of sources, including social media. IoT promises to streamline HR functions (like recruiting, workplace design, and succession planning) and impact individual employee performance (using badges and Fitbits to monitor healthy behaviors or productivity), thereby increasing the level and quality of HR services. These technologies are most powerful when properly implemented and tempered by a commitment to privacy and security. What follows is a brief description of each of the major technology trends that are directly relevant to human resources.

Social Media and Social Networking

While most people are using both social media and social networking by now, let's identify the differences between them. For the purposes of this book, *social media* is the suite of online platforms dedicated to community-based input, interaction, content-sharing, and collaboration, including video channels, blogs, wikis, and microblogs. Twitter, YouTube, and Pinterest are just a few examples. Social media is a way to transmit, or share information with a broad audience. *Social networking* sites include Facebook, Google+, LinkedIn, and many others and their purposes are the "creation and maintenance of personal and business relationships."[11] Having identified the distinctions between social media and social networking it is important to note that the lines have blurred between them. A case in point is the term social media network which is a combination of social media and social networking (e.g., tools like Twitter and Yammer provide the example). Conversely, you will note that social networks include many social media components such as blogs and other communication technologies. So keep an open mind in terms of categories of technologies, but be aware of their powerful applications. Further explanations and examples of HR social media and networking applications are embedded in subsequent chapters. For ease of use, we will combine the two into "social media" in Figure 2.2, Converging Technology Trends.

Big Data and Data Analytics

Big data provides the basis for data analytics. *Data analytics* is the process of examining large and varied data sets (i.e., big data) to uncover hidden patterns, correlations, trends, customer or employee preferences, and other useful information that can help organizations make more informed decisions.[12] It is used by HR to find trends and patterns in employee feedback, predict turnover and hiring needs, perform succession planning, identify pockets of increased employee engagement, and influence benefits-and-rewards decision making in addition to many other functions.

Mobile Computing

Mobile technology, or *mobile computing*, typically relies on cellular communication. *Mobile device* is a generic term that refers to the variety of tools that allow people to access data and information wherever they are using Wi-Fi or wireless technology. "Sometimes referred to as 'human-computer interaction,' mobile computing transports data, voice, and video over a network via a mobile device."[13] Included in the mobile computing category are drones, apps, mobile phones, and wearables. Many experts argue that the future of computer technology rests in mobile computing over desktop computing.

Cloud Computing

According to the National Institute of Standards and Technology, *cloud computing* is "a model for enabling ubiquitous, convenient, on-demand network access to a shared pool of configurable computing resources (e.g., networks, servers, storage, applications and services)."[14] Cloud computing "relies on shared computing resources rather than having local servers or personal devices to handle applications."[15] Different services, such as servers, storage, and applications, are delivered to an organization's computers and devices by third-party vendors. Typically, in cloud computing the hardware and software are not owned by the company using the service. Users pay for what they use as you would with any commodity, such as gas, water, or electricity. The idea is that savings are realized because the parent company doesn't have to make capital investments in hardware or software, allowing an "asset-light" approach. There are a variety of cloud offerings that we will discuss throughout this book.

Internet of Things (IoT)

IoT refers to the connection of devices (other than typical computers and smartphones) to the Internet. Cars, kitchen appliances, and even heart monitors can all be connected through IoT.[16] Dinah Wisenberg Brin writes that "a growing 'device mesh'—the network formed by wearable and mobile devices as well as sensors within other objects (which together make up the so-called Internet of Things)—is changing society and transforming business."[17] That is because the items in the mesh are not only connected, they also "learn," meaning that they respond and adjust as needed based on information gleaned from each other.

THE INTERSECTION BETWEEN THE TRENDS

Interestingly, each of these technology trends intersects with, relies on, and enables the others. So, you may have a mobile-enabled application that is cloud-based and relies upon social media and IoT to gather data which is then analyzed using big data analytics. These technologies are intertwined and provide impressive options for HR professionals. See Figure 2.2 for a graphic depiction of the intersection between the technologies.

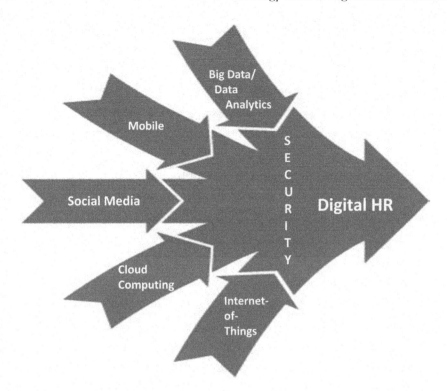

Mobile

Big Data/
Data
Analytics

Social Media

Cloud
Computing

Internet-
of-
Things

S
E
C
U
R
I
T
Y

Digital HR

Figure 2.2. Converging Technology Trends

Security

A caveat to all of the hype about these new trends is the very real need for security and privacy. As systems become more sophisticated, they may become more porous and permeable to those intending harm. It is critical to form a working alliance with your IT department to find solutions that mitigate potential vulnerabilities.

The HR department can also assist in preventing security breaches and cybercrime by implementing policies that defend and protect personal and sensitive information. Best practices include identity management, user authentication updates, encryption, regular system updates, and penetration tests to avoid potential security breaches. Interestingly, some organizations are using artificial intelligence (AI) to identify internal security risks. Through advanced mathematics and machine learning, AI can detect and highlight anomalous behavior in an organization's systems and networks, thereby protecting sensitive systems, network information, and intellectual property from criminal groups (or even malicious employees with access to the network).[18]

Trends and General Technologies

Throughout this text you will find examples demonstrating the applications of mobile computing, social media, big data and analytics, cloud computing, and IoT. Included are case studies from world-class organizations using innovative technology approaches that merge technology trends. Since cloud computing applies to every technology category in this text, a more detailed description follows. IoT, as a leading-edge technology will also be described further in this chapter. The other trends have their own chapters.

Cloud-Computing Options

A variety of cloud options exist and have developed over the past several years in the forms of public, private, and hybrid cloud computing. Public cloud computing is offered as storage space, bandwidth, and computing power. The organization is not responsible for managing a public cloud hosting solution. "Your data is stored in the provider's data center and the provider is responsible for the management and maintenance of the data center."[19] Many companies worry that a public cloud lacks security , but "even though you don't control the security of a public cloud, all of your data remains separate from others and security breaches of public clouds are rare."[20]

Private cloud, "also known as an internal or enterprise cloud, resides on [the] company's intranet or hosted data center where all of your data is protected behind a firewall. This can be a great option for companies who already have expensive data centers because they can use their current infrastructure."[21] This is a more secure option than public cloud but the cost may be higher, as the organization will need to maintain its own equipment.

Community cloud has a target set of consumers. Similar to a private cloud, it offers communal access to a population of users who have common privacy, security, and regulatory considerations. The cost is lower, but it requires multifaceted security. "Community clouds are often designed for businesses and organizations working on joint projects, applications, or research, which requires a central cloud computing facility for building, managing and executing such projects, regardless of the solution."[22]

Hybrid cloud is, as it implies, a combination of both the public and private cloud types and has similar advantages to a public cloud, including scalability (where you pay for what you use) and self-service, but is offered through a proprietary architecture. Some critical data reside in the enterprise's private cloud while other data are stored in a public cloud. Gartner indicates that hybrid cloud will be the approach of choice by 2020.[23]

The kinds of offerings that are available include, among other variations, *Software as a Service (SaaS)*, *Platform as a Service (PaaS)*, and *Infrastructure as a Service (IaaS)*. In SaaS, clients pay a periodic subscription fee in order to access software, including email, client relationship management and collaboration software, and enterprise resource planning. PaaS is essentially renting a computing platform, and is typically used by companies working with application development, decision support, and web-streaming services. IaaS provides "servers, storage and networking delivered as a service."[24]

There are numerous reasons to use cloud-based computing. The cloud offers 24/7 support, pay-as-you-use affordability, scalability, storage management, automation, a utility-based approach to usage, agile deployment, and device and location independence. These are compelling arguments in favor of cloud computing, creating an attractive alternative to the asset-heavy legacy systems. For organizations with employees scattered in multiple geographic locations, the flexibility in location is also appealing.

As with all technologies, security is an issue now more than ever. Concerns over cloud computing's vulnerabilities abound. Usually, as a technology matures it provides more solutions to mitigate the impact of vulnerability while retaining its initial characteristics, and cloud computing is no different. Though initially only the public cloud system was offered, there are now more secure options, including private and hybrid.

Of most interest from a security standpoint is the private cloud, which is generally considered more secure because the data in the cloud stays behind the company's firewall. Its other advantages include scalability and self-service.[25] It entails a higher cost than public, hybrid, or community clouds, and there is still some concern about security breaches, but it is most impermeable of all to external breaches.

IoT APPLIED TO HR

IoT will most likely impact the business landscape just as profoundly as the cloud. Although not yet quite as robust in its offerings to HR, IoT is predicted to provide undeniable benefits and spur new, ingenious applications. IoT is like a digital nervous system of mobile devices (including wearables) and sensors that connect devices with each other and with people.[26] Because of this network of connectivity, IoT can collect a lot of data.

IoT is and will be increasingly more useful to HR departments. Mobile phones and tablets can serve as central hubs in IoT because they provide easy access to people and their preferences. HR incorporation of IoT allows managers to provide continuous performance management by gathering performance data through IoT and providing immediate feedback. Employees will someday use IoT to identify the availability of flex workspaces because through IoT vacant rooms will be shown as "available." Attendance and location IoT trackers can monitor employee alertness on the job or provide time tracking to capture time and attendance data. IoT has endless, as yet untapped possibilities.

HR'S ROLE, NEW TECHNOLOGY TRENDS, AND THE WORKER

These five trends are called disruptive technologies for a reason. Keep in mind that new technologies impact workflow and work processes. The HR professional must manage the interface between the worker and the technology in order to assist with technology adoption. To facilitate the adjustment to new technologies and transition to new work processes, identify the impact on workflow and processes early and communicate these anticipated changes to employees. Then determine the target user's skills, knowledge, abilities, location, expectations, attitudes, and culture (audience characteristics) to identify technology skill gaps that can be addressed using training, job aids, or performance support. Doing this analysis beforehand will ensure a comfortable transition to the new technology.

The current technology trends sweeping organizations can change the entire way an organization does business. The adjustments required to implement these new technologies can cause major disruptions if ignored. However, by anticipating potential changes, studying preemptively, and preparing for and communicating changes and benefits to stakeholders, HR professionals can mitigate the potentially unsettling impact.

REGULATORY AND LEGAL ISSUES REGARDING TECHNOLOGY

HR should also have input regarding how an organization reaches legal and regulatory compliance. In some cases, there will be policy revisions required. The HR department will need to be aware of the regulations and how they will impact the organization. In order to successfully implement technology, organizations need to have reviewed and identified the intersection between the regulatory issues of the host country and the technology in use. Always err on the side of the more conservative interpretation of the law. Whether the prevailing law is that of the host country or the organization's home country, ensure that your organization carefully follows all guidelines that have legal ramifications. For example, some countries have relatively vague copyright laws, whereas US copyright laws are clearly outlined. Consequently, when designing courseware for an international audience, if the organization's headquarters are in the United States, abide by US copyright laws. Another example is if the host country includes time for midday prayers in their workday, but the country in which the organization is headquartered does not, abide by the guidelines of the host country and don't schedule conference calls or synchronous communications at that time.

As cybercrime rises, the issue of different laws between countries becomes increasingly important. Because developing countries often have fewer laws addressing cybercrime and law enforcement tends to focus on non-technology-related crimes, cybercriminals operate more freely. In failing to legislate or enforce laws related to technology, less-developed countries may inadvertently provide safe haven to cybercriminals. Keep these issues in mind and follow best practices in order to protect confidential data.

These examples demonstrate the expediency of knowing the technology-related laws of the host countries, especially for multinational organizations. Additionally, an understanding of the cultural mores for each country within a global organization plays a critical role in the success of the organization's technologies. Analyzing the specific culture within the organization and the impact the new technology will have on the target audience will also prepare the HR professional for the response to technology initiatives. Finally, answering the list of technology questions before choosing the technology and offering that important information to inform decision-making can have a positive impact on the process.

HR professionals can and should contribute to technology decisions, especially ones that involve the HR department and the people it serves. HR professionals bring a unique perspective to bear on any technology selection effort in that we can provide valuable input about the culture, business processes, employee disposition toward the technology, and the readiness of the organization for new technologies. It is our job to ensure that specific issues are addressed. HR professionals add value when we are informed; then we become irreplaceable members of the technology team.

Despite this knowledge, however, organizations are still missing out on the potential value HR professionals can offer in regard to technology. Deloitte released an infographic regarding research in global human capital trends in which they report that HR is still being left out of technology decisions, even ones impacting HR:[27]

- For example, in the Deloitte study, less than 36 percent of the organizations indicated that they included a member of HR as a technology advisor in technology decisions impacting the workforce.
- Only 4 percent of the organizations had a member of HR leading new technology efforts.
- Of the organizations involved, 65 percent reported that HR is only minimally involved in technology initiatives.

New technology will reach its maximum potential if it is guided into place by HR executives, managers, and practitioners who are knowledgeable about current technology trends and organizational and employee attitudes toward technology. In the following chapters we will examine many of the business applications for these disruptive technologies used in conjunction with other technologies. As HR professionals and business managers, we must participate in discussions about new technologies that effect the workforce because, ready or not, they are coming and they will have a direct impact on us.

End-of-Chapter HR Technology Strategy Questions

Considering your organization's overall business strategy and that of your HR department, as well as the needs of your employees, answer the following:

1. Which of these technology trends is your organization effectively using and how?
2. How could your organization incorporate "disruptive" technologies (cloud, mobile, big data/data analytics, social, and IoT) to enhance the overall HR technology strategy?

Digging Deeper

Bersin, Josh, Joe Mariani, and Kelly Monahan. 2016. "Will IoT Technology Bring Us the Quantified Employee? The Internet of Things in Human Resources." *Deloitte Insights*, May 24, 2016. https://www2.deloitte. com/insights/us/en/focus/internet-of-things/people-analytics-iot-human-resources.html.

Bughin, Jacques, Tanguy Catlin, and Laura LaBerge. 2017. *How Digital Reinventors Are Pulling Away from the Pack.* Survey, McKinsey and Company, October 2017. https://www.mckinsey.com/business-functions/digital-mckinsey/our-insights/how-digital-reinventors-are-pulling-away-from-the-pack.

Douglas, Genevieve. 2016. "HR Increasingly Adopting Cloud Technology." *Bloomberg News*, July 29, 2016. https://www.bna.com/hr-increasingly-adopting-n73014445636/.

Hashemi, Seyyed Yasser, and Parisa Sheykhi Hesarlo. 2014. "Security, Privacy and Trust Challenges in Cloud Computing and Solutions." *International Journal of Computer Network and Information Security* 8: 34–40.

Mercer. 2016. *The Journey to Digital HR: What Research Tells Us about Implementing a New HRIS*. N.p.: Mercer. https://www.mercer.com/content/dam/mercer/attachments/private/nurture-cycle/global-2016-hrt-journey-to-digital-hr-a4-mercer.pdf.

Schawbel, Dan. 2015. "10 Workplace Trends You'll See In 2016." *Entrepreneurs* (blog), *Forbes*, November 1, 2015. https://www.forbes.com/sites/danschawbel/2015/11/01/10-workplace-trends-for-2016.

Pelster, Bill, and Jeff Schwartz, eds. 2017. *Rewriting the Rules for the Digital Age: 2017 Deloitte Global Human Capital Trends*. London: Deloitte University Press.

Willer, Patrick. 2016. "How the Internet of Things Will Impact HR." *Talent Management and HR*, May 6, 2016. https://www.tlnt.com/how-the-internet-of-things-will-impact-hr.

CHAPTER 3

Converging Trends Using Social Media as an Example

TOPICS COVERED IN THIS CHAPTER

- Definitions of social media technologies

- Examples of HR uses of social media technologies

- Converging disruptive technologies

- Social media policy guidelines

- Case study of University of Colorado Health: using social media to communicate organizational identity

Converging technology trends are perhaps most evident in the area of social media. In this and subsequent chapters, when we refer to social media, we mean the technologies we use to reach out and connect with other humans, create relationships, build trust, and be there when the people in those relationships are ready to do business with our organization.[28] Social media comprises the tools for communication and collaboration. Or, as the *Merriam-Webster* dictionary defines it, social media includes "forms of electronic communication (such as websites for social networking and microblogging) through which users create online communities to share information, ideas, personal messages, and other content."

This chapter describes a variety of social media, provides examples, notes legal or regulatory issues, and offers some proven suggestions to apply these technologies to HR. The combination of social media and social networking will be demonstrated as a potent blend that can positively impact every stage of the employee life cycle including (but not limited to) organizational branding for recruitment, candidate sourcing, onboarding, social learning, knowledge sharing, employee engagement, and employee recognition. Additionally, the combined power of social media with cloud computing, mobile computing, IoT, and big data and data analytics are demonstrated. A case study, University of Colorado Health, offers an example of how one organization effectively leverages social media and social networking for organizational branding and recruiting. Finally, best practices for implementing a social media organizational policy and addressing potential legal issues will be presented.

SOCIAL MEDIA TECHNOLOGIES

The following social media technologies appear in this chapter:

- **Blog.** Derived from "weblog." It is the equivalent of an online journal.
- **Photo sharing.** A website where users share photos and videos (e.g., Flickr).
- **Podcast.** An audio or video file distributed over the Internet by syndicated download to portable media players and computers.
- **Vodcast.** The online delivery of video clips through web feeds.

- **RSS.** Really simple syndication, a format for delivering regularly changing web content such as news headlines and notices.
- **Wiki.** A website or similar online resource that allows users to add and edit content collectively (e.g., Wikipedia).
- **Mashups.** A combination of two or more data sources that have been integrated into one source. They typically consist of graphics, texts, audio clips, and video that have been sourced from various media sources, such as blogs, wikis, YouTube, or Google Maps, into a new product.

HR USES FOR EACH SOCIAL MEDIA TECHNOLOGY

There are standard uses for social media that HR typically employs; however, social media has recently been creatively implemented to do everything from sway public opinion to conduct pulse surveys to build relationships. What follows are recommendations that appear in the literature, but you can use your imagination and expertise to stretch the limits of this technology.

Blogs

A blog is usually a web-based publication similar to a journal. It is maintained by an individual who regularly enters, or posts, commentary, thoughts, and ideas much like a journal that is visible to the public. The writer may also include photos, audio, video, or graphics. These entries appear in reverse chronological order with most recent entries first. Usually, blogs are subject-oriented. Vlogs are blog sites that primarily use video, while linklogs are blogs that provide links to other sites.

For a sample blog, or to start your own blog, you may go to https://www.blogger.com or http://wordpress.com. To begin, you make a journal-like entry, and that original entry usually has a theme. Other writers then attach their comments by posting to the original entry. You can add a "tag" after the title of your post; the tag is a keyword or phrase indicating the topic of the entry. You may also see entries with similar key words by other bloggers by clicking on the word in the list of key words and phrases on the side of the screen. Bigger tag font size indicates increased use of that tag.

Blogs may be used for various HR purposes. As mentioned earlier, HR blogs typically revolve around topics or themes. However, HR is becoming more adventuresome and savvy about using blogs. The blog may be used to provide internal "customer service" to HR business partners (HRBPs). The employee inquiries that are filed can be analyzed for relevant content and recurring topics. Blogs can be used to provide expert information in a more interactive environment. A work-related blog can be used to convey organizational policy changes, explore new process improvements, and contribute to informal learning.

Blogs are generally opinions, which can be a drawback (unless they are from experts). Consequently, blogs should not be used as the final word regarding an important policy or legal issue. Blogs typically are not vetted to ensure quality and accuracy. Thus, you cannot always control what is learned and whether or not the learned information is correct when using internal blogs for HR purposes.

A *moblog* combines mobile technology with a blog. The content is posted to any blogging platform with mobile compatibility from a mobile device using mobile browsers or apps.[29] Moblogs offer readers real-time access to information. It is useful for travelers, tourists, and people who do not have access to desktop computing.

Photo Sharing

Flickr is one of many photo sharing websites. Flickr deals with visual content in the form of photos and videos. There is a collaboration feature in Flickr that allows individuals to participate in the organization of the photo and video files (not streaming video). Photos and videos are posted and visitors may add comments. These pictures can be printed in a variety of formats (such as postcards).

Many contributors allow use of their pictures through Creative Commons licensing, as long as you give proper credit. The original set of Creative Commons licenses all grant the same "baseline rights," such as the right to distribute the copyrighted work worldwide, without changes, at no charge.

Before organizations decide to use Flickr or other photo-sharing technologies, they must consider whether there is a need for copyright or legal permissions attached to the material they post. Of course, the photo sharing site can also be used for internal or not-for-profit purposes. For instance, team-building or morale-enhancing efforts may rely upon a display of (flattering) photos of the employees participating in team or organizational activities (although depending on the age of participants in group activities, you may need to get parental permission for pictures of minors).

Podcast/Vodcast

The podcast is a method of distributing digitized audio and video programs over the Internet. Using free recording software, anyone can create a podcast. The resulting audio files can be saved in different formats depending upon where and in what ways they will be used.

Additionally, there is also a video version of podcasting, called *vodcasting,* which uses video files distributed over the Internet and downloadable to media players and computers.

Podcasting has many uses. Audio is a powerful communication method, especially for narrative-based content. Interviews provide excellent content for podcasts. Role-play in podcasts or vodcasts can illustrate how to handle situations in positive, realistic ways. Storytelling also offers a powerful inducement to use this tool, as storytelling is a communication method that inspires, is believable, and is more interesting than simply relaying facts.[30] Educators and trainers find that podcasts can supplement, duplicate, or replace face-to-face lectures.

Really Simple Syndication (RSS)

RSS is a family of web-feed formats used to publish frequently updated digital content, such as blogs, news feeds, or podcasts. Users of RSS content use software programs called feed readers or aggregators. The user subscribes to a feed by supplying their reader with a link to the feed. The reader will automatically pull recently updated posts from those sites that you can read directly in the reader or on the source website by clicking the link provided. The reader then checks the user's subscribed feeds to see if any of those feeds have new content since the last time it checked, and, if so, retrieves that content and presents it to the user.

RSS has several advantages: Users can be notified of new content without having to actively check for it. For instance, updates to blogs can be automatically sent to users. The information presented to users in an aggregator is typically much simpler than most websites. This spares users the mental effort of navigating complex web pages, each with its own layout.

An RSS feed can be used behind firewalls. News updates, stock prices, and commodities can be sent out through the RSS. The business applications are obvious. For instance, for those working with banks or the stock market, this information is invaluable. Similarly, farmers could use an RSS feed to check future weather conditions or commodity prices. Organizations may find this technology useful for notifying clients or potential customers of important information. You can use https://feedburner.google.com to help you set up an RSS feed.

Wikis

Wikis can be sorted under social media or social networking; it fits into both categories. We have placed it in this chapter because it is a form of social media that can be used in portals and other communication venues. What is a *wiki*? It's "a website on which users collaboratively modify content and structure directly from the web browser."[31] It is user-generated content that allows contributions based on an author's expertise and knowledge. Ideally content may then be edited by subject matter experts who ensure its accuracy.

The best-known wiki is probably Wikipedia. This is a wiki that allows users to contribute to encyclopedia-like material. At the time of this writing, Wikipedia is overseen by a nonprofit organization that provides a platform for the world's largest online user-generated-content encyclopedia. The millions of articles included in Wikipedia are written by volunteers and experts around the world and edited by those with access to the site.

Businesses use wikis to gather, update, and maintain a body of information on an area of expertise. Because a wiki can be open to the public or restricted to members or employees, there are proprietary issues that may accompany its use. It is also valuable to organizations for retaining corporate information for collaboration and for training. Wikis can be used to organize the collective knowledge of the employees on a variety of topics from the esoteric (i.e., of value to a unique group within an organization, such as accountants or engineers) to the practical (such as advice for steps to apply for a grant at a university) to the mundane (for example, how to fix the copier if it is jammed). Embedded in the Microsoft Office 365 suite of products are cloud versions of Word, Excel, and PowerPoint that can function as wikis. These are familiar and easy to use because they are commonly available to anyone with user access to Microsoft 365. The practical use is that anyone with access rights can revise the shared materials from virtually any location.

There are, however, some cautions regarding the use of an internal corporate wiki for organizational purposes. Similar to public wikis, the most prevalent concern is security. This is because wikis are an "open" set of documents that are generally accessible to the employee base, which means they are vulnerable to misuse.

To avoid the theft and publication of private information, it is very important that organizations have clear policies in place regarding misuse of proprietary or confidential information, including any that might appear in a Wiki. A good reference on this topic is *Smart Policies for Workplace Technologies* (2017) by Lisa Guerin. The author provides sample policy statements and legal precedent.[32] While it is unlikely that policy statements will stop those with nefarious intentions, they do provide a legal position for prosecuting those who abrogate the policy.

Mashup

A mashup combines dissimilar types of information or disciplines. Another definition is provided by Lawrence: "A mash-up is the combination or mixing of content, ideas, or things from different sources to create something new or innovative."[33] What is interesting about mashups for HR is the suggestion that HR should start mixing up or combining ideas and resulting materials from internal departments and lines of business. This is a mashup in broad terms.

The above application implies that HR needs to be better integrated within the organization instead of retreating to our own kind, so to speak.

Mashing up in an HR sense means retooling ideas using different disciplinary approaches—for instance marketing and finance—and incorporating those viewpoints into one visual for HR purposes. An example of how this integration of departments, including HR, could be done is by presenting unique ideas from different departments on a topic of organization-wide interest, such as the dress code or flex time, into a single infographic.

CONVERGING DISRUPTIVE TECHNOLOGIES

Social media, as one of the major technology trends disrupting HR, overlaps with and converges with the other trends. Social media is made possible through the cloud. Social media is accessible from our mobile devices. A lot of data can be gathered from social media, and that data, when analyzed, provide insights into emerging patterns and trends. Gathering and initial vetting of data can be performed using IoT. All of these technologies are interdependent.

Social Media and Data Analytics

The importance and usefulness of big data gathered from social media cannot be denied. According to authors John Paul Isson and Jesse Harriott, social media can be a valuable source of information about employees within an organization or about external applicants considering joining.[34] Social media goes beyond the traditional barriers that separate personal life from the workplace. HR can use a social platform—one that many people visit several times per day for personal reasons—and redeploy the same media for HR purposes. Social media such as Twitter can be used for sourcing candidates and also for internal, organizational idea crowdsourcing, garnering feedback on a policy, or gathering innovative solutions to a common problem. The HR analysis of social media data, according to the authors Isson and Harriott, requires using social media, to "listen, connect, interact, engage, attract, source/select, develop/promote, and retain talent."[35]

Using social media sourcing for recruiting purposes can result in a better quality of hire and a shorter time to hire. Through social media you can connect with candidates who may not yet be looking for a new job. The social media information for potential candidates and relevant to hiring includes professional activities, conference attendance, white papers, skillsets, previous employers, and so on. This public information provides deep intelligence about the sourced candidate's professional profile.[36]

Social and Mobile

Employees—especially younger ones—expect HR services to be accessible on their mobile devices. With the rise of social media recruiting, or "social recruiting," the need for mobile access increases. Social recruiting involves leveraging a variety of social media tools to recruit talent. "Job recruiting has always been about networking; social media simply injects modern techno- logical networks into the tried-and-true formula."[37] Making the recruiting available on mobile devices increases its attractiveness to the intended audi- ence, most of whom use mobile devices. The social media side of mobile recruiting occurs when messages are pushed to the device by recruiters or social recruiting sites.

Social and Cloud

While cloud computing is relatively invisible to the user, the social media upon which HR now relies is made possible through the use of cloud com- puting rather than the older technologies, such as local area networks (LANs) or virtual private networks (VPNs). Thus, there is an invisible, but integral relationship between social media and the cloud.

Social Media and IoT

IoT is one global, digital nervous system of devices and sensors that can con- nect devices with each other and with people.[38] When connected to social media for HR purposes, IoT is particularly effective. IoT has been used— through tools such as mobile social media, badges, worn devices, or feedback kiosks—to analyze individual behavior patterns, verbal comments, and other data that assist companies in identifying key behavioral patterns. Social and IoT could be combined for a variety of positive purposes, such as rewarding emerging Centers of Excellence by providing conference rooms adjusted to their preferences at times of highest productivity. Determining those times would be a result of the IoT data gathering.

Of course, these tools could also be used against employees and that is the rub. There is a concern that monitoring behavior using IoT devices could be used for nefarious purposes such as surveillance of employees. This could cause employees to resist the use of advanced technologies or even undercut their adoption.[39] It is important to find positive uses for these technologies, applications that will benefit the employees, then tout those advantages.

TIPS AND TOOLS FOR EXPERIENCING SOCIAL MEDIA

- Blogs: https://www.wix.com/start/blog
- Photo sharing: www.flickr.com
- Tool for creating podcasts: https://www.podbean.com/
- How-to for vodcasts: https://www.youtube.com/watch?v=j4UWqTHtlZw
- RSS: www.reuters.com/tools/rss
- Wiki: www.pbworks.com
- Mashups: https://wordpress.org/plugins/social-media-mashup

SOCIAL MEDIA POLICY GUIDELINES

The purpose of creating private social media policies is to strike a balance between a congenial workplace that allows social media and one that protects confidentiality, security, and the employer's legal interests. A social media policy for your organization should include some of the basic principles below.[40] Remind employees

- That they are personally responsible for the content they publish on social media,
- That they must clarify that the views expressed in their posts are personal and not those of the organization,
- That they may not disclose confidential or proprietary information to any third party, and
- That they must avoid negative or defamatory statements.

University of Colorado Health: Using Social Media to Communicate Organizational Identity

Susan Swayze and Thomas Gronow

How do you communicate organizational identity in a fast-moving, technology-infused world? How do you communicate your organizational identity to current employees, future or potential employees, and communities? One organization, University of Colorado Health (UCHealth), utilizes social media platforms to communicate who they are and what they stand for, not only to a regional audience, but also to a national one.

UCHealth is a nationally recognized, eighteen-thousand-employee organization consisting of seven hospitals and more than one hundred clinics in Colorado, Wyoming, and Nebraska. UCHealth combines academic research and clinical care systems to provide next-generation medicine and treatment to more than 1.3 million patients each year. How does such a large and multifaceted organization espouse its identity far and wide? UCHealth utilizes social media and social networking vehicles, such as Facebook, LinkedIn, and Glassdoor, as channels that go beyond advertising positions to communicate organizational identity.

Historically, organizations would communicate information to their employees, customers, and stakeholders through print media, such as interoffice memos, pamphlets, and annual reports. With the popularity of the Internet came the digitization of these paper products. Such communication was one-directional—from the organization to others. These communication avenues were limited in that they largely targeted individuals and entities that were already connected to the organization. They did not provide a communication loop back to the organization, thus limiting useful feedback regarding how the organization is perceived by employees, customers, and the community.

UCHealth is undergoing rapid growth through expansion and acquisition; there were more than 4,700 external hires in 2016 and an acquisition in a new region. UCHealth leverages a social media presence as a medium to communicate its organizational identity to members of the communities that it currently serves and those in communities that it is moving into. Additionally, UCHealth's organizational identity is communicated to potential employees through social media. Specifically, social networking vehicles (such as Facebook and LinkedIn) and Glassdoor (a social media website for sharing information about organizations) provide insight into UCHealth—from what the organization is doing and producing to applicant and employee reviews of the organization.

With statements such as "18,000 employees, one mission" and "four regions, one mission," UCHealth draws consumers of information back to its mission statement: "We improve lives. In big ways through learning, healing, and discovery. In small, personal ways through human connection. But in all ways, we improve lives." With every post of a white paper, a career event, or a position description, UCHealth's organizational identity is disseminated along with the specific information. And when the post is liked or shared, UCHealth's identity is propagated exponentially.

UCHealth began its focused social media and social networking campaign in fiscal year 2015 (FY15) through its presence on LinkedIn, Glassdoor, and Facebook. UCHealth's presence on Glassdoor is a direct representation of the organization's identity. Through applicant and employee ratings and reviews, as well as UCHealth's contributions to the website including company information and photos, Glassdoor provides an inside look at what it is like to work at UCHealth. Through this targeted use of Glassdoor, UCHealth experienced a 25.2 percent increase in its overall rating between FY15 and FY17. As of this writing, UCHealth has the highest overall rating on Glassdoor, 3.88, compared to other major health systems in the Colorado market.

UCHealth's social media and social networking efforts effectively communicate its culture and values in the market. By utilizing social media, the organization enhanced its visibility far beyond the company website. In one quarter in FY17, the UCHealth Careers Facebook page received 72 new page likes, 258,393 impressions, 170,550 users reached, and 731 engagements, including reactions, shares, and comments. For the same quarter in FY17, UCHealth's LinkedIn page had 760 new followers, 140,685 impressions, 66,045 users reached, and 1,290 engagements, including likes, comments, shares, and clicks.

UCHealth has reaped the benefits of increased social media visibility. The organization experienced an 11.9 percent (7.4 percent for nursing) increase in applicant flow from FY15 to FY16 and a 29.4 percent (18.6 percent for nursing) in applicant flow from FY16 to FY17 since implementing its aggressive social media strategy. UCHealth experienced a 16.3 percent reduction in average time to fill between FY15 and FY17 (46 and 38.5 respectively). These statistics are a testament to UCHealth's social media presence. The visibility made possible by social media results in an increased number of passive candidates poised to apply for specific positions as they become available, thereby both increasing the number of applications and decreasing the time to fill vacant positions. Given that vacancies tend to cause overtime utilization for unfilled positions, extended vacancies are costly to the organization. A one-week reduction in time to fill saves roughly $1,000 in overtime utilization per full-time equivalent, making a low time-to-fill average monetarily advantageous.

Through social media and networking, UCHealth communicates its organizational identity to the public. Social media also serves as a conduit of information from the public back to the organization. In sum, UCHealth expertly marshals the power of social media to mediate the relationship between itself and the public sphere.

Susan Swayze, PhD, MBA, is an Associate Professor of educational research and an organizational development consultant. Thomas Gronow, MHA, EdD, is the Chief Operating Officer at the University of Colorado Hospital.

• • • • • • • • • •

Social media is varied and powerful. It can be used in many different ways. It can enliven presentations, personalize learning, equip novices with access to expert advice, and document innovations. Social media offers great opportunities, but with those opportunities comes responsibility. It is the responsibility of the organization to be aware of legal and regulatory issues surrounding social media in order to design effective stance policies about the use of social media in the workplace.

End-of-Chapter HR Technology Strategy Questions

Considering your organization's overall business strategy and the technology strategy of your HR department as well as the needs of your employees, answer the following:

1. How does your organization presently use social media for HR purposes? Is it an effective approach in your opinion? Why or why not?
2. How could your organization's social media policy and use be enhanced to align with the overall organizational and HR technology strategies?

Digging Deeper

Dessler, Gary, and Biju Varkkey. 2016. *Human Resource Management*. 14th ed. Noida, Ind.: Pearson.

Guerin, Lisa. 2017. *Smart Policies for Workplace Technologies: Email, Blogs, Cell Phones and More*. 5th ed. NOLO's Human Resources Essentials. Berkeley: NOLO.

Isson, Jean Paul, and Jesse S. Harriott. 2016. *People Analytics in the Era of Big Data*. Hoboken, NJ: John Wiley and Sons.

Milam-Perez, Lisa. 2017. "The Promise and Peril of 'Big Data.'" *HR Magazine* 62 (2): 72–73.

Milligan, Susan. 2017. "HR Then and Now." *HR Magazine* 62 (6): 38–41.

PART II

LEARNING MANAGEMENT

CHAPTER 4

Technology–Enabled Learning Environments

TOPICS COVERED IN THIS CHAPTER

- E-learning and online learning
- Online learning environments: a step beyond e-learning classrooms
- Learning management systems and learning content management systems
- Virtual reality
- VoiceThread
- Massive open online courses (MOOCs)
- Social learning
- Why use online learning?
- Video and learning
- Air Marshaller Training: A Serious Game
- Measuring learning

A wide variety of technologies are available to support organizational, team, and individual learning. Online learning environments offer a venue for distributing learning where learners are not co-located. Other tools—such as multimedia, audio and video components, VoiceThread, and gamification—enhance and enable learning. This chapter begins with an explanation of the shift from online learning to "learning environments." Next is a description of various learning tools, including massive open online courses (MOOCs). Finally, we will examine the emergence of gamification as a learning tool. This chapter highlights the positive impact of technology on instructional methodologies and the emerging emphasis on learner engagement, control, and empowerment.

E-LEARNING AND ONLINE LEARNING

For the purposes of this book, *e-learning* is defined as "education via the Internet, network, or standalone computer. E-learning is essentially the network-enabled transfer of skills and knowledge."[41] E-learning can be designed by programmers using programming code and hosted on a server, or it can be authored and hosted within a larger system called a learning management system (LMS).

Recently, e-learning underwent significant changes as a result of cloud computing coupling with competency-based learning initiatives. New products incorporate collaborative tools, and measurement is growing in importance in order to ensure that outcomes demonstrate actual value. The shift in e-learning is driving a more responsive and innovative approach, as well as new nomenclature.

The advancement of new learning technologies altered the very name from "e-learning" to the more frequently used "online learning." Online learning includes the initiative to create interactive learning environments. A *learning environment* is the context for learning, and the belief is that learning environments should be learner-centric (not instructor-centric). Online learning is customized to the intended audience using learning objectives to involve the learner. An example is Moodle's personalized learning environments.

Moodle and Sakai are two open-source LMSs. They are used around the globe as cost-effective solutions to online learning. The self-paced courses in

Moodle allow students to progress at their own speed. The environment is enhanced through various interactive features including video, audio, animation, games and images, videoconferencing capabilities, and simulations that engage learners. The media and game tools are built into the Moodle LMS. Furthermore, the built-in progress bar gives the user a sense of advancement through the learning.[42]

Edward Hess of Columbia Business School speaks about the importance of creating learning environments. He defines a learning environment as one that

> fosters intrinsic motivation and gives [learners] some autonomy and control over their learning. It's an environment where there are good role models for learning and creativity and where the style of teaching meets the diverse needs of learners. The learning process resembles a journey of discovery where the learner plays the main character and is encouraged to be creative and socially and authentically connected to the learning community. The learners experience a combination of positive support and positive challenges.[43]

Technology can be used to create the framework for a robust learning environment. Sophisticated learning tools and media properly implemented construct an effective context for learning. Multimedia makes possible the creation of complex learning environments.

ONLINE LEARNING ENVIRONMENTS: A STEP BEYOND E-LEARNING CLASSROOMS

So how does an online learning environment differ from the context of an e-learning classroom? Specifically, the technology allows for a student-centric experience giving the learner ultimate control. In so doing, the student establishes a *personal learning environment (PLE)* by developing personal learning goals, managing the method used to achieve those goals, and creating a customized context in which that learning will take place—ultimate control.

Another emerging approach to learning environments is the *flipped classroom,* which is instructor-designed but reverses what takes place in the learning context. As an example, in the flipped classroom learners may listen to or watch an instructor lecture outside class time, then come to the synchronous online session with questions (learner-centric) or do teamwork that involves the content of the lecture or other information provided outside class time (group learning). Often the methodology of the flipped classroom involves teamwork in a group setting rather than one-way lecturing. It generates more active learning using methods such as case work, data analysis, discussions, debates, or synthesis work. These methods provide opportunities to apply learnings. For a deeper understanding about the use of flipped classrooms and learning environments, see the texts in the "Digging Deeper" section.

As you update and refine your learning strategy, consider the following guidance regarding learner preferences in the twenty-first century: "[Learners want] systems that are as easy to use as everyday social media platforms and search engines.... Bring together a modern digital experience with all the face-to-face and multifaceted strategies that your employees need to succeed in their roles."[44]

LEARNING MANAGEMENT SYSTEMS AND LEARNING CONTENT MANAGEMENT SYSTEMS

The lines between LMSs and learning content management systems (LCMSs) have blurred. The LMS is the earlier version of the LCMS. Both still exist and serve different functions, although more current systems combine the two.

An LMS automates the administration of training events and records data on learner progress. An LMS can help launch e-learning courses. Through using the LMS, HR professionals or supervisors can observe patterns in courses enrollment and usage. They can track learner completion of required courses or select electives. The LMS can include classroom management, competency management, knowledge management, certification or compliance training, personalization and mentoring, and chat or discussion boards. With the advent of LMSs, many of the previously tedious logistics of course management can be handled online, as a self-service function.

The LCMS does not replace the LMS, but rather may interface with it or another larger system. The LCMS can be used to develop, maintain, use, and store instructional content. If designed properly, the LCMS can offer measurement and report results. The LCMS offers attractive features for both the instructor and the learner. The instructor can author materials, import existing materials, and develop, assemble, reuse, and repurpose content. The instructor can use the LCMS to access dashboards and generate reports. Maintaining and updating the courseware is also simple; no software programming skills are required. The instructor can deliver content in real time in multiple formats, even accommodating different languages (if language packages available). Learners can use the LCMS to pursue a customized learning approach, track their progress, collaborate with others, create a personalized web page, and document training completion.

VIRTUAL REALITY

Using advanced technology, a learning environment can replicate reality. *Virtual reality* (VR) is an artificial environment that is created with software and presented to the user in such a way that the user can manipulate and explore it. Virtual reality can take place on a computer, in a surround room, or using a mobile VR headset.

VR is being used by organizations to train individuals in certain skills by immersing them in an experience that seems real. The most successful implementations are occurring in healthcare, where VR is being used for skills training, phobia treatment, and surgery simulation. The military uses VR to learn new skills in a realistic but safe environment. Sports teams have been using VR to simulate the known plays or strategies of their opponents so players are prepared to react appropriately in the game.

VOICETHREAD

VoiceThread is an interactive venue that provides a refreshing alternative to linear training. VoiceThread allows the instructor to place collections of media (such as infograms, images, videos, documents, and presentations) in an online classroom. Learners attach their responses to questions posed by the instructors directly to them. VoiceThread marks where the response is placed to demonstrate what the comment relates to and maintains the responses so they are visible to all users and the instructor.[45]

MASSIVE OPEN ONLINE COURSES

Another radical development is the offering of *massive open online courses* (MOOCs). MOOCs are courses that are free and open to anyone in the world. The learning context is online. While MOOCs started in educational institutions, they have since extended to commercial and public organizations. Princeton is one of several educational institutions that offers MOOCs to more than 1.5 million students across the globe. For Princeton students, the MOOC offers supplemental materials in tandem with the content offered in the on-campus courses.

In the commercial setting, the applications for MOOCs extend beyond education to corporate training, where MOOCs offer everything from onboarding information and training, to professional development, to skill-building courseware, to branding, and even virtual recruiting. All is provided at little or no cost. MOOCs can be hosted on various platforms (including Coursera, FutureLearn, Khan Academy, Udacity, etc.). The goal of a MOOC is to provide learning without boundaries. The cost benefits are obvious.

SOCIAL LEARNING

With the advent of social media and social networking came the term social learning. Social learning is learning enabled by social media. It emulates the learning that occurs at conferences, in the office at the water cooler, and in open classes where the exchange of information and knowledge occurs naturally. According to Tony Bingham and Marcia Conner, it "combines social media tools with a shift in organizational culture, a shift that encourages ongoing knowledge transfer and connects people in ways that make learning enjoyable."[46] Opportunities for social learning should be embedded in online learning, but they often are not. The point of social learning is to create a context, like the water cooler, where ideas can virtually be shared using tools like blogs, social networking, wikis, Yammer, video of expert opinion, and the like. These may already be part of your LMS or you could incorporate into your HR portal or find another way to host intellectual exchanges.

WHY USE ONLINE LEARNING?

Online learning is increasingly relevant in the twenty-first century, as we conduct much of our personal and business dealings online. Many aspects of online learning appeal to organizations and learners alike.

Advantages of Online Learning

Online learning offers significant benefits to any organization that has the technology to support it and the wherewithal to invest in online learning infrastructure. Online learning is well suited to provide standardized training to an entire dispersed audience concurrently, especially if enabled by the cloud rather than over a Local or Wide Area Network (as conducted in past computer-based training). The materials on an e-learning website or LMS are easily updated to ensure they remain current, and well-designed e-learning can be highly interactive and collaborative. Online learning gives learners access to experts and visionaries they might not ordinarily meet. It is flexible, increases accountability because it is easy to monitor learner progress through the programs, and it can be adapted to the needs and learning style of the learner. Online learning is typically centered around the learners, not dependent upon the instructor. This change in the instructor role, as guide by the side and not stage on the stage, can be difficult for instructors unaccustomed to the approach.

Disadvantages of Online Learning

Online learning also has some limitations. For instance, the amount of learner control over online learning can create challenges for learners who are not self-motivated. Poorly designed materials can adversely impact learner participation. Off-the-shelf tools that are not customized to meet the learners' needs may diminish the power and appeal of online learning. Simplified courseware that eliminates higher-level thinking skills and the reflection necessary to perform management-level tasks makes e-learning unpopular among those who perform complex tasks that require judgment and evaluation. Organizations that use e-learning when they are not ready to support it often experience technology problems, which can undermine learning and cause the audience to react negatively. At the worst, e-learners will drop out.

VIDEO AND LEARNING

Video could arguably be called the preeminent media of the twenty-first century. As such, learners are accustomed to videos. The video site "YouTube has over a billion users—almost one-third of all people on the internet"[47] and video training is a reality in most organizations. Additionally, accessible online video forums have made it easier for organizations to distribute online training videos. The tools for creating engaging video have radically changed and enabled individuals to design beautiful, professional-looking videos on a reasonable budget.

Video and Training

For decades, video has been used for training purposes, but the approach to video training has recently changed. Current best practices for video design include

- Creating short chunks of information (i.e., the video should not be more than ten minutes in length);
- Keeping the video simple;
- Ensuring the video is deliverable to the bandwidth used by the intended audience; and
- Following the instructional design approach—Analysis, Design, Development, Implementation, and Evaluation (ADDIE).

A product like Camtasia is very effective for developing software training. It allows the designer to capture the keystrokes for using the software and add voice-over instructions for using the software in a video. Onboarding often presents the challenge of how to quickly get the new employee up to speed on how to use the different computer systems. Short training videos demonstrating the use of various systems can be developed in Camtasia and made available through the employee portal. This approach saves many hours of individual advising.

Videos as Storytelling

While both storytelling and video have long been used for instructional purposes, the approaches to both have changed over time. It in video form can have a powerful impact. Storytelling can be used for a variety of purposes, such as inspiring to action, teaching important lessons, explaining a task, setting a vision, or even defining a culture. When coupled with video, the story becomes even more persuasive. Christine Comaford of *Forbes* provides some clear guidance to ensure that your video story is effective:[48]

- Focus on the story customer by considering your audience.
- Reflect authentic situations.
- Shift from a problem or challenge to a desirable outcome.
- Make it value-oriented to demonstrate your own values.
- Ensure it stands up to the test (piloted in front of a subset of the intended audience).
- Edit appropriately.

GAMIFICATION

Another emerging online learning trend is the use of gamification for training. *Gamification* is the application of game elements and techniques to the nongame online learning process. Problem-solving is a key element of gamification; it can be used to motivate and engage learners.

Gamification has resulted in increased employee engagement in learning and team-building situations. It can be used to instill competition and involvement in what might otherwise be mundane learning topics. Gamification can motivate people through practical challenges, encourage them as they move through the levels of achievement, and incentivize them to do their best—all good learning outcomes.

Before you convert all of your training to games, however, keep in mind that gamification is not the answer to all of your employee engagement problems. Although studies demonstrate that some 75 percent of people in the workforce today are at least "casual" gamers, that doesn't mean that every topic can be addressed in this way or that everyone should be expected to learn through this tool.[49]

Return on investment (ROI) for gamification is hard to quantify. Maintenance of games is also difficult. So strongly consider your audience and the topic before using gamification as a teaching method. The best scenario for gamification is when the audience is accustomed to and energized by competition (e.g., sales or customer service). The topic should lend itself to levels of achievement (for instance, the learner has to understand one body of information before moving on to the next level). Gamification is effective in situations where the learner is seeking a level of mastery from which they can benefit (such as certification or an award).

In any case, elements of games can be adopted for increased learner involvement. Use the competitive and social aspects of games to enhance learning experiences. One example of gamification is the air marshaller training by Designing Digitally Inc.

• • • • • • • • • • •
CASE STUDY

Air Marshaller Training: A Serious Game

Andrew Hughes

Designing Digitally Inc. was looking for a creative way to integrate the Microsoft Kinect into learning to show potential clients the possibilities of the device. Designing Digitally Inc. decided to teach end users aircraft marshalling signals utilizing the Kinect. Rather than just present the information to the learners, they wanted a solution that was immersive as well as fun and would teach the learner what signals are needed to direct the pilot handling the plane.

After a detailed research and analysis phase, Designing Digitally Inc. determined to create a serious game that was fun, yet educational. This innovative game teaches learners how to do the air marshal signals and then puts them into a competitive experience where they have to maneuver the airplane through an obstacle course. The learner is timed and tracked to see how well they did compared to their peers.

This game shows potential clients the possibilities for using the Kinect in training. This is a fun and positive learning experience for the end user. Overall, it has been an eye-opener for trainers throughout the world and the demo version is being used by

Designing Digitally Inc. at conferences to show the effectiveness of games and simulations in the workforce.

Andrew Hughes, President of Designing Digitally, founded Designing Digitally Inc. in 2006; it is an e-learning and serious game development firm that creates fully customized learner retention solutions for various types of industries.

• • • • • • • • • • •

MEASURING WORKPLACE LEARNING

Big data and analytics are technology trends impacting HR today. Big data is the vast amount of web-based, mobile, and sensor-generated information. Analytics are the methods that specialists use to draw meaning from the data. Through data analytics, we can discover which learning resources employees seek out, which are used most often, and which employees recommend to others. Further, to the extent that social learning is incorporated in the online learning, we can track who is relying on specific in-house experts to get answers and solve problems, what questions are being asked, and indicators of learning gaps to uncover areas where training is needed. Of course, successful use of data analytics relies on an organization's data storage capabilities, analytics software, use of metrics, and qualified individuals to perform data analysis, all of which are necessary to successfully gather meaning from big data.[50]

In summary, organizations can employ a number of methods and tools to enhance online learning by creating learning environments using video, gamification, MOOCs, and social learning hosted in LMSs or online. Additionally, data analytics can be used to identify trends in learning online. Clearly there is a wide variety of ways to make your learning available and meaningful by using technology.

End-of-Chapter Technology Strategy Questions

Considering your organization's overall business strategy, answer the following:

1. What is your organization's learning strategy and how does your organization effectively (or ineffectively) utilize technology to enhance learning?
2. How could your organization integrate some of the training technologies presented in this chapter to enhance its overall HR technology strategy?

Digging Deeper

Bingham, Tony, and Marcia Conner. 2015. *The New Social Learning: Connect. Collaborate. Work.* 2nd ed. Alexandria: ATD Press.

Hess, Edward D. 2014. *Learn or Die: Using Science to Build a Leading-Edge Learning Organization.* New York: Columbia Business School Publishing.

CHAPTER 5

Learning–Technology Selection

TOPICS COVERED IN THIS CHAPTER

- Technology selection and LMSs

- Case for cloud-based LMS

- Cost benefits of online learning

- LMS vendor selection and evaluation

- Regulatory considerations

- Workplace legal policies for instructional and courseware designers

- Learning management systems and talent management

- Cornerstone OnDemand case study: learning and so much more

Learning happens in a variety of contexts both formal and informal. The learner's location should not limit learning. If we broaden our definition of the learning context to include any place where one is capable of learning, we can also expand our view of who is an active learner. John Kotter says that people must learn continuously in order to lead or even stay relevant,[51] so it is in everyone's best interest if those responsible for establishing learning opportunities in the workplace make them accessible, and continue learning themselves.

Technology challenges the notion that learning must take place in a classroom, as it can extend learning to anywhere the learner has Internet or telecommunications access. But not all learning situations are the same, and there is no one learning technology that will satisfy every learner. Several considerations must influence the selection of online learning technology.

TECHNOLOGY SELECTION AND LEARNING MANAGEMENT SYSTEMS

Learning design fundamentals should impact the instruction system design. These points pertain primarily to online learning offered through an LMS. Of course, there will be variations depending upon the course content but keep the basics in mind. Design learning for both online and mobile delivery using the following Universal Instructional Design (UID) principles:[52]

- Aim for simplicity, so create shortened courses called "courselets." These deliver well to a mobile device, maintain learners' attention, and can be reused in a variety of contexts.
- Support a community of learners by incorporating social interaction into the course using blogs, wikis, video-enabled groupware conversations (such as GoToMeeting or Skype), discussion forums, chats, and learner-run projects.
- Provide equitable use by designing for the lowest technological common denominator.

Beyond those basics, some other relevant design principles impact online and mobile learning (m-learning):

- Create products that combine technologies (mashups). This approach builds an environment rather than a sterile courseware.
- In larger classes, limit groups to twenty or fewer students to avoid unmanageable discussion threads.
- Provide easy access to key aspects of the course; do not involve multiple screens in accomplishing a single task.
- Use infographics, metaphors, pictures, and other visuals to enliven the courseware.
- Place navigation, function, and content buttons, as well as instructions and graphics, in predictable places; keep them there throughout the course and across courses in the same program.

There are also a few essential guidelines for instructors in online courses:

- Prepare for and enable the instructor's role change from sage-on-the-stage to guide-by-the-side.
- Establish behavioral norms early, or have learners do so, and be sure that they are clear and agreed upon.
- Provide clear, prompt, and frequent feedback because there are no other cues from which learners can receive the message.

CASE FOR CLOUD-BASED LMS

A possibility that is available on the market today is cloud-based LMS. One mass media corporation, which we will call MediaMogul, is using a cloud-based LMS. MediaMogul combines industry expertise with technology, using cloud-based learning to deliver training to decision-makers in a variety of industries.

MediaMogul identified a need to train and develop its global sales team. The information in the courseware had to be current and accessible for decision-making, and also needed to align with the fast-paced information sharing that the team was accustomed to. Among other features, MediaMogul wanted their LMS to be mobile accessible. Further, it had to adapt to the languages of global employees. They chose an SaaS enterprise

LMS, and now use it to train all of their sales representatives. Learners can set up individualized training plans to ensure that they receive exactly the materials they need. The SaaS feature allows the global team to access materials from any location at any time using a mobile device. MediaMogul reports that the cloud-based LMS reduces the cost that would typically be incurred to train everybody to an equal level of knowledge using traditional, face-to-face, co-located methods.[53]

This chapter provides guidance on the best practices for selection of a learning management system (LMS). Different configurations are examined for incorporating learning management either as a module in a larger human capital management system or as a standalone system. The case study provides a powerful example of one very robust LMS within the Cornerstone OnDemand talent management system.

Cost Benefits of Online Learning

The most obvious savings are the savings on travel, housing, food, and so on when a course is offered online. But when you consider LMS features compared to face-to-face course delivery, other cost savings become apparent. In short, increased savings occur when learning options are offered for both online and mobile. The development and hosting costs vary based upon the LMS costs, whether prepackaged or customized learning modules are chosen, and how sophisticated the technology is (e.g., costs of video or gamification or text). In-house custom instructional development is typically more costly than prepackaged, commercial, off-the-shelf products.

Some organizations use open-source LMSs, such as Sakai or Moodle, for greater cost savings. As mentioned earlier, open-source software is computer software distributed with its source code available for modification, including a license for programmers to change the software in any way they choose. Of course, there are limits to the kinds of courseware people will put on an open-source site, but required courses or courses that deal with generic topics, such as providing performance feedback, are often legally offered in an open-source environment. The cost savings result from the fact that it is generally free to download and modify. A further attractive feature of open-source and proprietary LMSs is that most are also mobile accessible, which means participant access the courseware from either a PC or mobile device.

Modifying courseware to be mobile-friendly does incur expense. The temptation will be to cut corners and allow existing courseware to be accessible through a mobile-accessible portal, also known as "porting." This does not work well. The specific limitations of mobile handheld devices hobble visibility, increase download times, and interrupt the user learning experience if courseware is unaltered, which will foster a negative reaction to the whole learning experience. Mobile courseware must be designed for delivery to mobile devices with accommodations made for screen size, bandwidth, and so on.

TIPS AND TOOLS FOR SELECTING AN LMS/LCMS VENDOR

- Establish your budget parameters.
- Assemble a team.
- Agree within your team on the evaluation criteria.
- Involve the team in preparing the request for information.
- Involve the IT department so that you are prepared to answer questions about user system requirements, installation, maintenance, ownership of imagery, and so on beforehand.
- Do your vendor research and invite at least three vendors to demo their solutions, which will be the basis for your request for proposal.
- Make your selection.

REGULATORY CONSIDERATIONS

Over the years, as online instruction has matured, legal standards and best practices for the design and distribution of web-based instruction have emerged. Most off-the-shelf learning management systems developed in the United States comply with Scalable Content Object Reference Model (SCORM) standards. These standards for interoperability—promoted by the Advanced Distributive Learning Initiative of the US Department of Defense—specify a set of technical standards for e-learning software products. SCORM tells programmers how to write their code so that it is compatible with other e-learning software. It is the industry standard for e-learning interoperability.

Specifically, SCORM governs how online learning content and LMSs communicate with each other. Even if your organization is not US-based, these standards are helpful.

A shift away from SCORM may be coming, driven again by the mobile learning trends and also by the changes in our work culture. Those in learning and development find themselves serving as experience designers, curators, and consultants. The curator role resulted from the need to organize massive amounts of learning information. A *content curator* is the person accountable for gathering, organizing, and updating relevant information available to employees, typically through a portal. Content includes but is not limited to courses, articles, videos, photographs and drawings, blogs, research reports, case studies, and other types of digital learning objects.

Aviation Industry Computer-Based Training Committee (AICC) standards are emerging requirements that apply to the development, delivery, and evaluation of training courses delivered via technology (more often than not, LMSs). AICC is an international association of technology-based training professionals that develops training guidelines for the aviation industry. Most current LMSs are both SCORM and AICC compliant.

Many consider Tin Can Application Programming Interface (API) to be the next generation of SCORM compliance standards. In short, Tin Can API will allow content and systems to interface without being constricted by some of the older standards inherent in SCORM. Tin Can API sets the scene for the integration of a variety of multimedia and programmed instruction. SCORM, AICC, and Tin Can API are standards that enable the instructional designer to host and deliver complex learning products in a variety of ways on a variety of platforms.

WORKPLACE LEGAL POLICIES FOR INSTRUCTIONAL AND COURSEWARE DESIGNERS

Creators of learning materials, typically instructional designers, find it very easy to incorporate articles, documents, and scanned textbook pages into an e-learning or multimedia product. It is therefore also quite easy to break US copyright law. Important copyright principles and laws that affect the design of e-learning courseware for US organizations include the fair use doctrine and the TEACH Act. Abiding by these laws is a major concern for instructional designers today.

The important point here is that no one should profit from the unique published works of another author without obtaining that author's permission to use those ideas. Most relevant to online learning are the requirements for posting copyrighted materials online. Fair use permits limited use of copyrighted materials without the permission of the copyright holder under certain circumstances, but the user is typically required to obtain permissions for copyrighted materials if the materials are used for profit. You do not need permission to use works in the public domain because these works are not protected by copyright.

LMS AND TALENT MANAGEMENT

We are now finding that the options for LMS selection extend beyond a standalone system. Many organizations select an LMS that is part of a larger talent management or human capital management portfolio. The learning management function is integrated with other HR functions, such as recruiting, performance management, employee relations, payroll and benefits, and pensions and departures. Cornerstone OnDemand is an integrated talent management system that includes a robust learning management system. The following case demonstrates how Cornerstone OnDemand, the company, uses its own product for learning management.

. . . .
CASE STUDY

Cornerstone OnDemand: Learning and So Much More

Kimberly Cassady

The desire to fulfill one's potential isn't merely generational; it's human nature. Imagine if every employee in a company was given the opportunity and the means to contribute their best possible performance. For Cornerstone, this is more than a compelling idea—it's the very foundation of the company. Cornerstone was founded on a belief that a lifetime of learning and development is fundamental to growth—for both the employee and the organization. The company created what is today one of the world's leading cloud-based learning and human capital management/talent management software solutions. From training and collaboration, recruitment, and onboarding, to performance management, compensation, succession planning, people administration, and analytics, Cornerstone is there at every phase of the employee life cycle. Internally, Cornerstone uses its own software for recruiting, learning, connecting, compensation, and performance.

Cornerstone makes heavy use of its learning and engagement tools. A full suite of training tools through the LMS includes instructor-led training (ILT) sessions, with adaptations to the system to incorporate different types of ILT trainings, such as massage or cooking classes. The learning and development (L&D) team is always exploring and expanding the use of cohorts and learning communities. Cornerstone uses cohorts to manage its leadership development program and introductory training program. Participants in the leadership development program complete an e-learning curriculum as prework, then progress to an in-person seminar which is followed by a two-month, inquiry-based learning experience, all driven through cohorts. In the past three years, more than one hundred managers globally have engaged in this program. Its blended-learning approach to leadership development includes an online course, an in-person course, and a community element.

Additionally, L&D executives are spearheading a full learning catalog overhaul in order to drive better overall engagement with the employees. As L&D leaders start to focus more heavily on push-pull and predictive learning, employees can now find relevant training that excites them. The company has replaced lengthy, irrelevant courses with actionable microlearning courses. Reporting functionality makes catalog editing significantly easier, because it is based on employee ratings.

While there are organizations that try to force a collaborative environment, Cornerstone believes it must be organic. Connecting employees through learning communities and cohorts is driving cultural engagement, promoting internal values, and providing business benefits. It takes commitment and internal promotion and marketing to keep a community going. Communities for business applications and learning are the two strongest areas at Cornerstone. Business-focused communities can cut time from administration. Social recognition programs also do well internally and complement the company culture.

Implemented in September 2012, the Applicant Tracking System (ATS) is one of the top areas where Cornerstone maximizes the capabilities of its talent management solution. Over the past two years, the company has moved to 100 percent utilization of online job applications globally, which means that candidate profiles and job applications are not only in one database but also providing real-time data, enabling the team to increase efficiency and effectiveness by analyzing year-over-year results. Using its Interview Manager (IM) tool, which manages interviews through Microsoft Outlook and tracks them within the ATS, the company has decreased its sales time to hire by ten days. Additionally, it has increased its offer acceptance ratio from 50 percent to 87.5 percent after making adjustments based on data gathered within the system that illustrated process gaps in various divisions. Because of the high volume of recruiting done within the technology and engineering team, an evaluation of interview time was needed to evenly distribute employee time spent in interviews. Using the IM-enabled tracking of interviewers' time spent in interviews and away from their work resulted in process modifications that decreased manager interview hours and improved the manager-candidate experience. ATS has enabled Cornerstone to measure the percentage of hire rates across the business to identify challenging divisions and roles, and hiring managers who are hesitant to make a hiring decision. The company is also using its own system to promote internal mobility by accessing employee information about skills, competencies, and career interests to match employees with other job openings at the company.

Cornerstone is a pay-for-performance organization and goes through an annual competency and goal-based performance review with recommended raises focused on performance accomplishments. Among its benefits, the compensation tool enables equitable performance practices with its increase recommendation guidelines and configurable budget monitoring.

Through the performance process, the company is making strategic changes in how it manages. Cornerstone has identified key competencies and offers learning content to complement it. General core competencies for the organization include "smart," "dependable," "visionary," "teamwork," and "focused on client success," along with two to three functional competencies for each department.

Using compensation to facilitate their pay-for-performance program provides compensation managers the flexibility to equitably reward employees on the basis of merit. Organizationally, significant process efficiencies have been created since performance ratings, score calibrations, compensation plan submissions, approvals, and reporting are all managed within the solution.

Clearly, Cornerstone OnDemand satisfies a wide range of HR functions, with learning as a foundation for the entire suite of offerings. As a global learning and human capital management software provider, Cornerstone OnDemand is pioneering solutions to help organizations realize the potential of the modern workforce.

Kimberly Cassady, Vice President of Talent for Cornerstone OnDemand, drives all internal talent initiatives for Cornerstone's global workforce, including talent acquisition, talent operations and compliance, learning and development, global engagement, compensation and benefits, and facilities and administration. She directly leads a team of more than forty talent practitioners. Kim brings more than fifteen years of experience in human resources and operations leadership.

In this chapter we examined LMS components, the cost benefits of online learning, selection of learning technologies, and regulatory and legal considerations. We concluded with a case study of an organization, Cornerstone OnDemand, that effectively uses its own Cornerstone Learning product and the rest of the talent management suite to handle HR functions. In the next chapter, we will examine options for mobile learners.

End-of-Chapter Technology Strategy Questions

Considering your organization's HR technology strategy, answer the following:

1. How should your organization's current HR technology strategy impact the learning technology selection within your organization? Are any refinements needed to the HR technology strategy?
2. How could technology empower your employee training and development strategy and which technologies would you suggest?
3. How can cost benefits be realized through your learning technology choices?

Digging Deeper

Bingham, Tony, and Marcia Conner. 2015. *The New Social Learning: Connect. Collaborate. Work.* 2nd ed. Alexandria: ATD Press.

Burbach, Ralf. 2015. "Training and Development Issues and Human Resource Information Systems Applications." In *Human Resource Information Systems*, edited by Michael J. Kavanagh, Mohan Thite, and Richard D. Johnson, 411–51. Thousand Oaks, CA: Sage.

Hess, Edward. 2014. *Learn or Die: Using Science to Build a Leading Edge Learning Organization.* New York: Columbia Business School Publishing.

Quinn, Clark N. 2014. *Revolutionize Learning & Development: Performance and Innovation Strategy for the Information Age.* San Francisco, CA: John Wiley & Sons.

CHAPTER 6

Mobile Learning

TOPICS COVERED IN THIS CHAPTER

- M-learning design

- M-learning environments

- Productivity and mobility

- Mobile computing: Legal ramifications

- Workplace policies

- Fortis m-learning case study

HR has a new role in the twenty-first century. The good news is that organizations finally realize that the human resources management function is vital to their overall success and profitability. Since employees are every organization's biggest asset and since HR interfaces with employees from prehire to separation, HR is involved from beginning to end with an employee's experience within an organization. That is a lot of responsibility. As a result, the roles of twenty-first-century HR professionals have changed to include new competencies. As stated in Chapter 1, HR behavioral competencies include business acumen, ethical practices, leadership and navigation (with political finesse), HR expertise, relationship management, consultation, global and cultural effectiveness, communication, and critical evaluation. Communication and critical evaluation pertain directly to technology skills,[54] and both of these skills can be supported and enhanced by mobile technology.

Mobile computing impacts the field of learning. For instance, executives, small business owners, and those with HR responsibilities find themselves needing to use new methods to consistently incorporate formal learning, informal learning, and leadership development methods in the workplace. (Mobile learning, or m-learning, may be the answer to address all three.) In order to be effective, HR leaders must be aware of and use theories of learning and instruction that fit mobile technology.

We know that those without access to high-speed connections are increasingly at a disadvantage. This disparity has been labeled "the digital divide," referring to the gap in opportunities between those who have access to high-speed, high-quality connections and those who do not. This opportunity gap can be said to stem from the fact that most recent technologies are focused on network-enabled tools that are often reliant on broadband Internet. However, in many ways, mobile technology bridges the gap by making learning platforms accessible from mobile devices like cell phones. Now the leading-edge goal in business is to be mobile friendly. Top-quality learning and development products can be delivered to mobile devices, thereby reaching a broader audience than the desktop-based online audience and overcoming the divide.

In this chapter, we will refer to the use of a mobile device (smartphone, cell phone, or tablet) for learning purposes as m-learning. M-learning provides learning beyond the boundaries of developed nations to many developing nations and people around the globe.[55] This is no small achievement and it is one that you need to know about, especially with regard to the impact on employee learning and development. We address m-learning design guidelines, explaining what they are and how they differ from standard principles of instructional design. Additionally, we explain how augmented and virtual reality can be used effectively as mobile learning.

M-LEARNING DESIGN

In 2016, an estimated 62.9 percent of the global population already owned a mobile phone, and it is forecasted to continue to grow, rounding to 67 percent by 2019.[56] Given the exponential increase in the number of mobile phones and the increased hours of usage, forward-thinking HR professionals must realize the advantages of using mobile devices for work purposes, specifically for training or training support. If most people in the workplace are using mobile devices, why not incorporate mobility into learning activities? Or, better yet, why not deliver training to the mobile device?

For the last decade, instructional designers have been developing an approach to deliver training on mobile devices. One of these design approaches, Universal Instructional Design or UID, is impacting the design of all online instruction, not just m-learning.[57] UID has many associated principles. UID principles provide an effective approach to the design of learning based on the technology, audience, context, content, and pedagogy. These design considerations can be further specified as follows:[58]

- **Technology category.** This requires a review of the technology for compatibility of the devices the intended audience uses, the access method, organizational policies to support the technology, and metrics for measuring the impact and results of the technology.
- **Audience.** Requires knowing and being able to describe the intended audience, what their learning needs are, what interests them, and the technologies that they use for their workplace priorities.
- **Context.** Requires examination and identification of the environmental conditions for learning, formal or informal learning opportunities,

possible distractions, corporate norms for technology usage, and cultural norms regarding the technology.

- **Content.** Addresses the match of the instructional design to the content, incorporating active, problem-based, or project-based learning that is both challenging to the learner and suited to the content.
- **Pedagogy.** Requires determination of the role of the instructor and student and what must be accomplished. Otherwise known as the instructional goal. Ideally this approach assumes the instructor's role as guide-by-the-side rather than sage-on-the-stage, giving the learners more control by allowing them to analyze, synthesize and construct their own, new learnings.

UID impacts the structure of the course and the curriculum. M-Learners need to know how each learning courselet fits into a whole course or curriculum. You can help them identify this by making the structure of the course clear with a content plan of the whole course at the beginning of each courselet. Similarly, it is important to make the objectives for each courselet clear at the start so that learners have an overall indication of what will be covered. Content that is applicable to mobile learning includes short, two- to three-minute videos, a few frames of content, and simple interactions such as polls or short quizzes.

HR professionals can use their power and influence to help others see the possibilities and think outside the box, especially in regard to mobile learning. The first step is to examine the technology options—including smartphones, cell phones, tablets, and hand-held computers—that provide alternatives to PC-based access to learning.

M-learning delivered to mobile devices allows students to learn from a variety of locations where online, PC-based courseware may not be accessible. Often, areas that have no broadband Internet will still have telecommunications capabilities. The availability of learning courses and courselets on mobile devices in situations where there is no broadband Internet extends learning. People can obtain information and learning materials on their mobile devices almost anywhere and at any time.

M-LEARNING ENVIRONMENTS

We talked earlier about learning environments, but how do those environments differ when adapted for mobile devices? Mobile devices offer an alternative virtual learning environment. At the time of this writing, there are about four and a half billion cell phones in use around the world (with some individuals owning more than one phone).[59] The reliance on mobile technology makes it logical to explore cell phones and other mobile technologies as viable delivery systems for training media. This is not a well-defined domain yet, so keep the UID principles in mind and innovate!

Interactive Multimedia

Multimedia refers to a combination of text, audio, pictures, animation, and video. Interactive multimedia is multimedia that uses digital, computer-based systems to respond to the user's actions. One of the benefits of multimedia is that the enriched sensory involvement of an interactive multimedia program increases learner motivation and engagement. Additionally, the use of multiple modalities accommodates a broader array of learning preferences for a wider range of learners. Also, multimedia is more realistic: the use of photographs, audio, and video makes the content concrete. When case studies and simulations are included, the training situations become even more realistic. Text and captions can be used for multilingual materials. Multimedia can be used individually, in groups, or in pairs with the net effect being an improvement in the learners' digital literacy.

While our focus is not on the design and development effort, it is important to have a general understanding of how multimedia programs are created. As with any instructional design effort, there is an extensive amount of analysis needed to specify the purpose and goals of the program, expected learning outcomes, the audience characteristics, the best delivery technology, and necessary system requirements for the target audience. Everything, except for the system requirements, is standard to the instructional design process.

As mentioned earlier, there are a number of technology issues to examine, and the agreed-upon solutions to those challenges impact the design and development of multimedia products. It may be necessary to develop multiple versions of the program that run on different types of system configurations. Remember those who may not have access to smartphones or high-speed Internet in this situation because multimedia requires bandwidth that some do not have.

The designer dictates some of a multimedia product's level of interactivity. Nevertheless, the bulk of the design for interactivity should be drawn from learning theory, strategies, objectives, and content. Multimedia forms that are easily adapted for mobile learning include podcasts and vodcasts. More sophisticated multimedia requiring special mobile devices include virtual reality and augmented reality.

Podcasts and Vodcasts

Podcasts and vodcasts are audio and video files, respectively, that are distributed via the Internet or telecommunications to a computer or handheld device. Podcasts are easily created using open-source software. (An example is Ardour at https://www.ardour.org.) Vodcasts are videos stored in digital form that you can download from the Internet and play on a computer or an MP3 player.[60] The recorded products can be exported in a format that is compatible with the device on which the podcast or vodcast will be run.

Virtual and Augmented Reality

Virtual reality is a set of images and sounds produced by a computer that seem to represent a real place or situation.[61] For training purposes, virtual reality has now come into its own, especially when it is adapted for a mobile device, specifically a headset. The headset is designed for the purpose of recreating the visual experience. It is perfect for training situations that might be difficult or dangerous to perform or expensive to recreate and involve activities that can be simulated.

Augmented reality uses the existing environment and overlays new information on top of it.[62] The designer will use a special programming language to integrate animation and digital information based upon the location of the user (when designed for a smartphone). The user will identify a marker, such as a barcode image, then the software "analyses the marker and creates a virtual image overlay on the mobile phone's screen."[63] This approach is reliant upon a smartphone.

Virtual and augmented reality continue to evolve in both the technology and its creative usage. Mobile augmented and virtual reality are developmentally in early stages.

PRODUCTIVITY AND MOBILITY

Using mobile devices to enhance workplace productivity is obviously of great interest to employers and HR professionals. There are many advantages to using mobile devices for increasing workplace efficiency. In an article written on this topic, Boris Dzhingarov states that mobile technology encourages social networking and communication from basically anywhere.[64] Coupled with the power of tools such as LinkedIn, Twitter, Yammer, and Facebook, mobile technology clearly enhances networking and networking can increase employee engagement, learning, and development. But what else can it do?

Mobile devices and mobile learning can be used to increase innovation by improving information sharing, enabling immediate feedback on ideas and products, and supporting more responsive, immediate customer service. Mobile technology allows customers to use their mobile devices to access and interact with distributors using their mobile devices, which provides a marketing advantage.[65] Mobile technology offers increased portability and flexibility, access to business processes to streamline procedures, reduced commute time, and a hiring pool that is diversified.[66] What's not to like? Furthermore, organizations can maximize the inherent strengths of mobility by building those assets directly in their m-learning courseware.

Another way to increase worker productivity is through mobile access to Dropbox and SharePoint technologies, both of which allow users remote access to files previously placed within those services. Dropbox is a cloud-based service that provides the first 2 gigabytes (GB) of storage for free; for additional storage, payment is required. It is named for the repositories used by banks, post offices, video stores, and libraries that allow people to drop items off securely. SharePoint is a Microsoft product that also allows remote access to a secure online place where users can store, organize, share, and access information from any device through a web browser.[67] It is also cloud-based.

MOBILE COMPUTING: LEGAL RAMIFICATIONS

There are issues and legal ramifications inherent to mobile computing. For employees, the concerns differ from those of the employer. In the case of bring-your-own-device (BYOD) systems, employees are most apprehensive about their loss of privacy. The information on their mobile devices is no longer their own if they use the devices for business purposes. While this is hardly a new concern, it may be the foundation for a legal quagmire.

For the employer, security issues are the problem. Employers' major concerns are about the vulnerability of sensitive data on employee mobile devices. If that device is lost or misplaced, others can have access to sensitive data that may include customer personal information, customer feedback, contracts, competitive data, intellectual property belonging to the company, invoices, nonpublic corporate financial data, marketing information, and so on. Mishandling any of this information could result in loss of intellectual property, compromised private information and other breaches that can result in embroilment in legal actions, and other negative repercussions. It is therefore best to have a clear mobile-use policy in place.

A great source on these types of policy and legal ramifications for HR professionals is the BLR (Business & Legal Resources) report that is available with a membership at BLR.com.[68] Additionally, your in-house legal department will have insights on these critical matters and the SHRM bookstore offers many useful resources as well. Always review legal and policy ramifications before introducing a new technology such as mobile computing in the workplace.

Workplace Policies

The BYOD policy has become a very important topic. For some HR professionals, the savings that could potentially be realized are not worth the security risk. Again, be sure to consult your legal department regarding any questions you may have with any new technology.

Be sure the policy takes into account the individual requirements of each role. Next, identify who has access to sensitive data. Then decide where your employees are on the risk continuum from a low-risk to high-risk profile. Address each of these vulnerabilities in your overall policy.

A very important article by Lannon and Schreibe provides clear guidance about how to design a good BYOD policy. Your policy should address[69]

- How to separate workplace from personal information on the device;
- Which devices will be permitted and supported and what employees can access from their devices; and
- Based on job description, which employees may or may not use their own devices for work.

In addition, you must be certain to

- State the policy clearly and include a provision of the employer's right to access, monitor, and delete information;
- Delineate allowable employer monitoring;
- Provide notice when information will be deleted from the device; and
- Collaborate with IT, risk management, operations, and legal counsel to ensure that your policy complies with current guidelines.

. . . .
CASE STUDY

Mobile Healthcare Certification Course at Fortis Healthcare, India

Sunil Omanwar

Fortis Healthcare is among the largest healthcare service providers in India, with approximately 4,700 operational beds in 45 healthcare facilities across geographies and a total potential bed capacity of over 9,500 beds. Fortis's mission of saving and enriching lives is backed up by the presence of key specialties in care, such as cardiac sciences, neuroscience, orthopedics, renal sciences, gastroenterology, oncology, and pulmonology, treating around 260,000 domestic and 15,000 international patients every year. It has a strong team of 3,000-plus clinicians with approximately 17,000 employees overall.

In the organization, there are 330-plus Fortis sales professionals engaged in ensuring that patients and the community choose Fortis for distinctive patient care. While classroom training programs were developed and conducted to address a few training objectives, the majority of the training objectives were identified as candidates for m-learning. This required building a learning curriculum that (1) catered to and reinforced respective hospital unit standards and (2) offered customized training in areas pertaining to topics such as anatomy, diseases and disorders, treatments, procedures and surgeries, terminologies and key terms, clinical excellence, medical equipment, and technological advancements.

Training challenges for sales folks included cost, speed, richness, reach, and accessibility, since sales folks are always on the move. Prior to the m-learning solutions, the sales force dealt with

- A lack of existing customized content. Specifically, there was a need for training on medical specialities that catered to the Fortis brand while reinforcing product knowledge requirements.
- Little access to learning environments. The Fortis sales force is mobile and dispersed across various locations over a significant geographical spread. Conventional classroom training was not an effective, flexible, or cost-effective solution.
- Little time to gain standardized product knowledge certification. The sales force team had to be trained in a short time without compromising learning richness and content.
- Short attention spans. The sales team had difficulty paying attention to traditional learning methods (classroom studies, reading, lectures, etc.).
- Continuous or on-demand tracking, reporting, and assessment scores.

The L&D team collaborated with in-house Fortis subject matter experts (i.e., clinicians) to create a standardized yet unit-specific learning curriculum, then the L&D team partnered with Qustn Technologies to deploy a mobile-based learning platform through which the courses and corresponding assessments could be accessed from a smartphone.

The mobile-based platform solution helped the organization mitigate the previously stated challenges. Launched in December 2016 to the entire sales team, the new m-learning courseware incorporated learning modules and online assessments where a specific certification standard (scoring 80 percent or above in all the assessments under a specialty) must be met. The mobile-based solution offered easy and instant access, bite-sized modules, and flexibility for self-pacing the learner experience. The short, interactive learning experience (case studies, simulations, practice quizzes, and visual components) with easily navigated features and functionalities aided learner engagement and knowledge retention. After successful completion of each medical specialty, the participant received an automatically generated certificate of completion. This immediate feedback resulted in enhanced motivation and a sense of achievement within the sales force. The m-learning modules have subsequently been integrated into the existing LMS as e-learning and are currently being used both for reinforcing and refreshing key lessons to the existing team, and educating new hires in the Fortis sales force.

The following outcomes demonstrate the effectiveness of the Fortis m-learning approach:

- Course completion rate: 91 percent
- Total number of users: 303
- Number of application downloads: 299, or 99 percent of the sales force
- Course (medical specialty) completion rate: 91 percent, meaning that of the 1,656 courses assigned, 1,507 were completed

These statistics clearly demonstrate the efficacy of the m-learning approach for the Fortis Healthcare sales force.

Sunil Omanwar, Vice President of Learning and Organization Development for Fortis Healthcare in India, has over two decades of experience in organization learning, leadership development, and talent management. He is also a founding member of the Institute of Group Facilitation.

● ● ● ● ● ● ● ● ● ● ●

This chapter addressed a variety of mobile technologies used for m-learning. The m-learning design section provided guidance on how to create powerful m-learning instruction. We examined workplace productivity and considerations for use of mobile devices, legal ramifications, and guidelines for policy development with regard to mobile devices.

End-of-Chapter HR Technology Strategy Questions

Consider your organization's overall business strategy and that of your HR department, then answer the following:

1. What are your HR's established mobile policies and procedures?
2. How can current mobile technologies in use within the organization be leveraged to support mobile learning and employee development? How would you measure the success of such?
3. How should HR's mobile policies and procedures be updated in light of the considerations proposed in this chapter?
4. How does your HR department integrate mobile into its HR Technology Strategy? In what innovative ways could the HR Technology Strategy be improved to include mobile computing?

Digging Deeper

Beetham, Helen, and Rhona Sharpe. 2013. *Rethinking Pedagogy for a Digital Age: Designing for 21st Century Learning*. 2nd ed. New York: Routledge.

Elias, Tanya. 2011. "71. Universal Instructional Design Principles for Mobile Learning." *International Review of Research in Open and Distributed Learning* 12, no. 2 (February): 143–56.

McQuiggan, Scott, Lucy Kosturko, Jamie McQuiggan, and Jennifer Sabourin. 2015. *Mobile Learning: A Handbook for Developers, Educators, and Learners*. Hoboken, NJ: John Wiley & Sons.

Schadler, Ted, Josh Bernoff, and Julie Ask. 2014. *The Mobile Mind Shift: Engineer Your Business to Win in the Mobile Moment*. Forrester Research. Cambridge, MA: Groundswell Press.

Traxler, John, and Agnes Kukulska-Hulme. 2016. *Mobile Learning: The Next Generation*. New York: Routledge.

CHAPTER 7

Training or Performance Support?

TOPICS COVERED IN THIS CHAPTER

- What is a performance support system?

- Mobile performance support systems

- Considerations before incorporating performance support into your technology strategy

- Training and mobile performance support

- The user interface and performance support

- Mobile performance support in practice

- Groundwork of Denver, a case study using mobile performance support

Gloria Gery was the original guru of performance support systems, previously called electronic performance support systems (EPSSs). For more than two decades, Gery advocated for performance support through her various contributions on the topic, including extensive research, real-world applications, and personal experience. We'll begin this chapter with Gery's definition of a performance support system (PSS), then we will leap forward to the twenty-first century. The shift will capture the resurgence of performance support and its current attributes for workplace application. We'll examine the impact of mobile- and cloud-enabled performance support with some tips and tools regarding its practical use in HR. Finally, you will see an example of how that performance support can positively impact an organization in the case study regarding mobile performance support. Keep in mind that—as with each of these technologies—integrating performance support into the overarching HR technology strategy is of the utmost importance.

WHAT IS A PERFORMANCE SUPPORT SYSTEM?

Gery defined a PSS as a system that provides users with "individualized online access to the full range of...systems to permit job performance."[70] The emergence of performance support tools heralded major changes in learning and knowledge management while providing alternatives to standard face-to-face training. Currently, the wave of technology trends (mobile, social, cloud, big data, and IoT) has made performance support systems more available and powerful than ever. As of this writing, "we are now seeing an emergence of PSS technologies and associated methodologies that are proving astonishingly effective [for learners] to access the information they need in support of practice activities...and reduced time to proficiency."[71]

Why has the PSS become so important? The faster pace of business demands shorter "time to proficiency" when employees need to learn new skills.[72] The PSS emerged as a natural fit to assist employees and shorten the time involved in learning how to do their jobs with the desired level of competence in a complex workplace with increasing demands. It also reduces reliance on training as the ultimate solution for performance improvement.

Benefits of a Performance Support System

Performance support can provide assistance in a variety of ways because it provides workers with access to the equivalent of training as they are doing the work. Typically, performance support helps workers do the job while they are on the job. There are many advantages to this approach. Through purposeful design, the performance support system or PSS can contain knowledge embedded in the interface, support resources, and system logic, making it a multifaceted tool. The PSS is used during natural work situations, so the worker learns on the job with feedback that occurs in the context of doing the job. Through use of a PSS, the worker can access helpful information and tools without breaking the flow of the task. A well-designed PSS can provide layers of functionality to accommodate a diverse population including adaptation for language differences, level of proficiency at the task, and so on. Some of the tasks can also be automated through the PSS. In fact, the PSS attributes offset and in some cases totally replaces the need for training.

MOBILE PERFORMANCE SUPPORT SYSTEMS

Recent demands in the workplace require organizations to make these performance support systems available on mobile devices. The advantage to this is that the mobile device is something that workers will typically have with them. So, the worker can receive information at the time of need, while doing work, on a device that is always at hand—the mobile device. The benefits of mobile performance support systems cannot be overemphasized, as they provide[73]

- On-demand knowledge when and where it is needed,
- Information available on numerous platforms so any device can access it,
- Audio and video capabilities to access product information and other knowledge, and
- Offline storage so that information can be stored and invoked as needed.

In Gery's own words, performance support should "fuse learning and doing to enable immediate performance with minimal external support" and "to institutionalize best practices on an ongoing basis, all of the time...

to enable people who don't know what they are doing to function as if they did."[74] Mobile performance support accomplishes all of the above with the added benefit that it is delivered on a device as small as a smartphone.

CONSIDERATIONS BEFORE INCORPORATING MOBILE PSS IN YOUR TECHNOLOGY STRATEGY

There are considerations, the answers to which determine whether or not a mobile PSS is appropriate for the employees in your organization:

- What devices are workers accustomed to using both at work and in their personal lives?
- What kind of access do potential users have?
- What are the technology policies of your company?
- What devices will enable access to the knowledge, create the knowledge, or provide (push) the knowledge?
- How will you measure activities and results?

When to Use Mobile Performance Support

It is appropriate to use mobile performance support under the following conditions: when accuracy is critical, the work task is performed infrequently, there are multiple decision points or steps (that the person is unlikely to remember), the work task is error-prone, the procedures and tasks are changing, the worker has a low level of literacy, and/or training is unavailable.

Schadler, Bernoff, and Ask provide clear guidance regarding mobile performance support, saying that it should benefit both the employee and the employer. For the employee, consider the following: The mobile support should deliver a service that improves an employee's experience. It must run on the employee's preferred device. It should help the employee accomplish goals quickly and deliver a better experience, and it should provide the information an employee needs to complete a task. For the employer, the mobile performance support should enhance worker productivity. Elimination of steps, or process simplification, is a plus because it saves time and ultimately money.[75] When all of these converge, you have a powerful, cost-effective alternative to training.

When Not to Use Mobile Performance Support

Conversely, as mentioned earlier, there are times when a PSS is not the right solution. For instance, mobile PSSs should not be used in instances where it would cause the worker to seem less credible, such as performing a sensitive surgery to an awake patient. Do not use mobile performance support in instances where speed is critical (because it may be hampered by mobile), such as a life-or-death emergency medical technician procedure. Avoid using or designing mobile performance support for situations that are unpredictable or novel work processes. Remember that in context, support may have distractions that will detract from user focus. If distractions are present, mobile support may not be the answer.

TRAINING AND MOBILE PERFORMANCE SUPPORT

If performance support systems do what they are supposed to do, they diminish the need for training. However, another paradigm is to use training and performance support together. There is no need to choose between instruction and performance support; mobile performance support can work in tandem with instruction. The workplace requires employees to remember an expanding amount of information and demands that workers take on ever-increasing responsibilities; performance support and training can assist them with both. The primary objective of the PSS is to help the learner complete a task as rapidly and error-free as possible.

Mobile performance support can be an augmentation of training. As such, "organizational learning moves from being a training event to which employees need to be invited, to something that happens automatically as employees seek assistance on-the-job from PSS."[76] If training is the answer, then the learning content can be offered as self-paced, on-demand instruction through a PSS. The result of this approach is to give employees access to resources at their own pace rather than at pace dictated by an instructor. Classroom time can then be used for hands-on skill practice, or it can be sequenced and presented as online or mobile learning.

THE USER INTERFACE AND PERFORMANCE SUPPORT

In the past, most online performance support relied upon a graphical user interface (GUI) because it was PC-based. As both PCs and mobile devices move toward a natural user interface (NUI) approach so does performance support. A *GUI* is where you use a metaphor or icon to represent a task, idea, or topic. An example on your mobile device may be the envelope for email, a microphone for voice transmission, or a camera for taking a picture. A GUI is invoked typically by touch or a mouse. The *NUI* invokes a different approach so it is directly consistent with your natural behavior. For instance, when you swipe with one finger, you scroll through pages or you move content from one side of the screen to the other. The gesture itself corresponds to the action you are performing. This is a particularly interesting difference when using performance support. For mobile PSSs, make the support as easily accessible as possible using the devices that your audience typically uses.

Bill Gates (principal founder of Microsoft) made the following statement about NUI: "With NUI, computing devices will adapt to our needs and preferences for the first time and humans will begin to use technology in whatever way is most comfortable and natural for us."[77] Gesture interaction relies on movements that come naturally, such as swiping with a finger on a mobile device or PC to move a page forward from left to right while reading—a common movement that replaces the GUI approach of pressing a page down key. Voice-activated tasks—such as those used with GPS technology in order to get directions on a Garmin or a smartphone—provides an example of another type of NUI. The advantage of the NUI is that it is less disruptive to the workflow of the person using mobile performance support.

MOBILE PERFORMANCE SUPPORT IN PRACTICE

Scott McCormick provides some practical examples of how mobile support can be used. Take note of this because it provides you with some quick aides to produce mobile performance support. Some that are relevant and not too costly to design include cue cards or flashcards; video explanations or demonstrations; searchable applications such as contacts, checklists, and maps; checklists for things like safety steps and repairs; process maps or decision trees to solve problems; tips that are relevant to performance; and assessments that use a natural interface where a question is posed and the respondent can answer by voice.[78]

Wearables, such as Google Glass, smartwatches, and Fitbits, can also be used to provide the end user with a wealth of valuable data based on the environment, sight, sound, movement, and context. They enable delivery of live support, coaching, augmented reality, and context-monitoring for live adjustment (such as recalculation based on location indicated by a GPS embedded in the mobile device).[79]

TIPS AND TOOLS FOR USING MOBILE PERFORMANCE SUPPORT

- Use mobile performance support when you need immediate task implementation with minimal external support.

- Involve representatives from different parts of the organization in developing mobile performance support.

- Design applications so that they work on any device (making them "device agnostic" applications).

- Enjoy savings over the life of the system in the form of reduced time for the worker to perform operations, reduced overtime, reduced calls to the helpline, fewer training costs, and less downtime.

CASE STUDY

Groundwork Denver: A Case Study Using Mobile Performance Support

Dr. Joel Selanikio

Groundwork Denver is a nonprofit organization that partners with lower-income communities to improve the physical environment and promote health and well-being. "Groundwork teams consist of young people ages 12–24; the majority are high school age and are recruited from Denver public schools to apply. Each Green Team has 8–11 members and a project leader."[80]

The volunteers plant trees, improve parks, clean up rivers, insulate houses, promote biking, grow food, and coordinate hundreds of volunteers to help. To orchestrate events and initiatives, the leaders of Groundwork Denver turned to Magpi. Magpi is a mobile data collection app whose "mobile technology provides easy data collection, communication, and collaboration in the field—wherever that may be. It lets users create mobile forms and messaging applications, and then send those to any cellphone, smartphone, or tablet. For Groundwork Denver's Green Team . . . project supervisors can collect real-time data on their cellphones," which is helping Groundwork Denver work more efficiently: "Groundwork Denver team members can now go paperless when collecting field data about the environmental revitalization and conservation work they do; everything from planting trees and cleaning up streams, to gardening, building playgrounds, and habitat restoration. More Magpi and less paper use means Groundwork Denver is doing its own part to contribute to a green environment while still collecting all the 'green data' they need."[81]

For Groundwork farm supervisors, for example, that means more precise tracking of six thousand tomato plants that the team is planting. Magpi makes it easier to plan out on a mobile device, using specific forms, what needs to be accomplished each day of the project without lugging around notebooks and files.

"It's definitely nice and tangible to see what we've done," says Shane Wright, Youth Program Director for Groundwork Denver. "With Magpi to help us collect data during our projects, we actually know how many tomatoes or trees we planted, and can document the progress and the outcome. It's really streamlined the process, and we're able to catch a lot of things that were slipping by us before."

Since Groundwork Denver began using Magpi last year to support some thirty-eight environmental projects in the Denver metro area, Wright says they've seen significant improvement in the amount and accuracy of information they collect.

"This will be our best year of data collection," says Wright. "In the past I used a calendar and my 'chicken scratch' notes which was less than good data collection; I often had to go back and guesstimate. But with Magpi our outputs are much higher. Now we can code, share our progress, and build surveys based on our reporting requirements. This helps with annual and quarterly reporting because we can say exactly how much we accomplished."

And no matter what area of the city a project is in, Magpi is reliable. Even in areas where cell phone reception and Internet connectivity can be poor, Magpi is effective.

"We like the fact that our team can collect data whether they have an Internet connection or not," says Wright. "We're already helping our fellow Groundwork Trusts grow their capacity to capture and track their outputs and impact using Magpi technology."

"We are very proud to partner with Groundwork Denver and to see Magpi's impact in helping them reach their goals," said Rose Donna, COO of Magpi. "Groundwork Denver's success demonstrates yet again how useful Magpi is across sectors, and in demanding environments."[82]

Dr. Joel Selanikio, Chief Executive Officer at Magpi, is an award-winning physician, TED speaker, inventor, emergency responder, and consultant working in the fields of technology, healthcare, entrepreneurship, innovation, AI, big data, child health, global health, and disaster response. He is the winner of the Wall Street Journal *Technology Innovation Award for Healthcare, and the $100,000 Lemelson-MIT Award for Sustainable Innovation.*

A performance support system can be a cost-effective way to provide the right information on location to the user at the right time. When delivered to a mobile device, the mobile performance support can enhance productivity. While the design is labor intensive and can be expensive, the potential rewards—improved performance for the labor force as a whole, a shorter time for new hires from hiring date to productivity—are worth it.

End-of-Chapter Technology Strategy Questions

Considering your HR department's technology strategy, as well as the needs of your employees, answer the following:

1. In what ways could mobile performance support enhance your organization's HR technology strategy?
2. Review the list of conditions under "When to Use Mobile Performance Support," then determine which (if any) of those conditions apply to your organization. In your opinion, what training could be replaced or enhanced by mobile performance support?

3. If your organization already uses mobile performance support, is it accomplishing its purpose to streamline targeted processes and help employees be more efficient? If not, how would you improve the support tool, the process, or both?

Digging Deeper

Quinn, Clark N. 2014. *Revolutionize Learning & Development: Performance and Innovation Strategy for the Information Age*. San Francisco, CA: John Wiley & Sons.

Rossett, Allison, and Lisa Schafer. 2007. *Job Aids & Performance Support: Moving from Knowledge in the Classroom to Knowledge Everywhere.* San Francisco: Pfeiffer.

Schadler, Ted, Josh Bernoff, and Julie Ask. 2014. "The Workforce Shift." In *The Mobile Mind Shift*, edited by Forrester Research, 131–65. Cambridge, MA: Groundswell Press.

Traxler, John, and Agnes Kukulska-Hulme. 2016. *Mobile Learning: The Next Generation*. New York: Routledge.

PART III

TALENT MANAGEMENT

CHAPTER 8

Handling HR Talent Management Functions

TOPICS COVERED IN THIS CHAPTER

- Using an HR system for talent management

- Cloud-enabled talent management

- Human Resource data

- HR system technology trends

- Wyndham Hotel gamification for onboarding

- Business process reengineering

- Laws governing HR systems

The single, integrated HR systems that handle the employee life cycle—from recruiting and onboarding through separation and benefits—are varied, each with a different set of attributes and functions (see Chapter 9). We will refer to these computer systems as "HR Systems" from this point forward. In this chapter, we will examine HR functions and the role that an HR system or integrated systems play in capturing and storing reliable HR data. The case study demonstrates how a large, hospitality firm uses technology to handle onboarding in a unique and engaging way.

The important learning from this chapter is that there is no single, "right" HR system that suits every organization. Further, there is no single HR system that performs every HR function well. Your organization's mission and vision as well as its technology infrastructure, legacy systems, and evolving technology needs are unique. Therefore, HR technology solutions should be designed to meet the needs of your organization.

USING AN HR SYSTEM FOR TALENT MANAGEMENT

Talent management is the process of attracting, developing, retaining, and deploying the best people.[83] Talent management optimizes every phase of the employee life cycle. Originally, human resources relied on a variety of systems for talent management. As organizations have realized the value and importance—even the earning power—of their employees, the pressure on HR to provide increased automated capabilities escalated. Additionally, with the advent of cloud computing, a variety of systems emerged. In Chapter 9 you will see a typology for different HR systems (Table 9.1). In short, they can be categorized by functional offerings with the HR fundamentals handled by a Human Resource Information System (HRIS), and the next levels adding more sophistication in the types of analytics, including predictive and planning capabilities, and other functions. Talent management systems, the topic of this chapter, are those that deal with every aspect of the employee life cycle. They are more often than not cloud-based.

CLOUD-ENABLED TALENT MANAGEMENT

Talent management is an HR-specific term that is key to understanding HR's role. We groom and develop talent. The combination of talent management system functions with cloud-computing provides a powerful alternative to the asset-heavy legacy systems which require more than one system to perform the same functions as a talent management system. The cloud version of talent management is a viable alternative to using several systems to handle the full range of HR functions.

Benefits of cloud computing include improved user experience, more efficient innovation, shorter deployment times, easier upgrades, lower costs, and less IT dependency from the oversight viewpoint. Cloud-based HR systems offer an asset-light approach because another organization owns, maintains, and upgrades the legacy systems. From a financial accounting viewpoint, cloud computing is used on demand, such that an organization can consume as much or as little of a service by using only the needed functions. The financial ramifications are that you pay for the services that you use. The organization leases a preset amount of computing power over an annual period, budgeted similar to telephone or electrical expenses. A cloud-based talent management system does not require a large initial capital investment.[84] Cloud services are configurable and flexible.

Cloud delivery inspires buyers to focus on cloud solutions for all HR functions. However, instead of employing one massive suite of cloud services (as in an ERP solution), you can use the HR cloud-computing system (such as an HRIS, talent management system, human capital management system, or HR management system) for the most-used and critical functions. Some functions such as payroll or recruiting can be handled by standalone systems that should be integrated with the HRIS/TMS/HCMS/HRMS. The point is that there is a lot of flexibility in how a cloud-based HR system is configured.

HUMAN RESOURCE DATA

The advantages of a cloud-based HR system are many, not the least of which is a *single source of (data) truth*: "the practice of structuring information models and associated schemata such that every data element is stored exactly once."[85] In association with this concept is *single version of truth*, "a technical concept describing the data warehousing ideal of having a single, centralised database."[86] Together these concepts provide the advantages of an

HR system. A disadvantage of using several legacy systems is that information is dispersed across those systems, making data collection fragmented and the data potentially unreliable.

The cloud-based HR system has the appearance of a single-tier model, like the mainframe systems of the 1980s. The Internet acts like the mainframe supercomputer, providing the application run-time environment.[87] Typically there is one database for the cloud-enabled system, the result of which is that all of the functions in the single system are integrated. This is a tremendous asset that serves as the basis for many of the advanced, predictive analytics embedded in the HR system.

Data Cleansing

Many HR departments fear the nightmare of transferring data from legacy systems to a new cloud-based HR system. This reticence keeps the organization from progressing and benefiting from all of the reports and valuable information available in such an upgrade. However, the concerns must be addressed. In order to move data from a legacy system or systems to a single system, there is a challenge of cleansing the data to make it accessible and usable. This is not an easy or fast process. "Data scrubbing, also called data cleansing, is the process of amending or removing data in a database that is incorrect, incomplete, improperly formatted, or duplicated."[88] This procedure can be performed both within a single and between multiple sets of data, manually (where possible in simple cases) or automatically (in complex operations). When switching from using a variety of systems and different protocols for storing data to using one system with its unique protocols, there may be what is called dirty data. This can be caused by a number of factors, including duplicate records, incomplete or outdated data, and the improper parsing of record fields from disparate systems. To correct the data and make them usable, data cleansing must occur.

Methods used for data scrubbing follow a variety of approaches. One is the extract, transform, load (ETL) methodology, where old data are reloaded into a new data set using a conversion software. Data cleansing uses statistical analysis tools to read and audit data based on a list of predefined constraints. Data that violate these constraints are put into a workflow for exception data handling. Another data cleansing approach is extract, load, transform (ELT), where the system automatically performs the data transformation when loaded.

Big Data and Data Analytics

The role of big data becomes immediately apparent as we examine the functions of an HR system, the big data that is available by having an integrated system, and resulting analytics capabilities. Looking at this topic from the viewpoint of the employee life cycle provides further insights. Isson and Harriott point out the importance of this approach: "Developing a model that enables you to track your candidates and new hires from the first time they hear about your company through the employee life cycle will help you keep your fingers on the proverbial pulse of your talent and enable you to better manage your retention activities."[89]

Isson and Harriott, however, point out the need for *integrated*—connected, not standalone—systems to access data for analysis. We cannot overemphasize the fact that properly integrated HR systems are an ultimate source for extracting meaningful data. If they are not integrated, you cannot be assured of the integrity of the reports.

What are people analytics and why should you care? *People analytics* "[bring] together a company's employee-related data to solve specific business problems in such areas as sales productivity, retention, fraud, and customer satisfaction."[90] Rising globalization, competitive recruitment, decreased employee loyalty, and digital technology's impact on labor make hiring and retaining qualified employees more difficult.[91] Predictive people analytics provide information that could mitigate possible turnover.

HR Systems, Metrics, and Financial Data

HR metrics and data are critical because the reputations of organizations can rise and fall based on data and metrics. Since HR typically does not develop measures demonstrating its strategic business value, it becomes a target. And yet HR is the only department that is involved with employees through the entirety of the employee life cycle. The Balanced Scorecard is a performance metric used in HR's strategic management to measure and provide feedback to organizations about the organization's financials, customers, internal business processes, learning performance, and growth.[92] But in a recent survey of chief financial officers, less than one-third of those polled trust or use the data received from the HR team when making business decisions.[93] That is really scary. What does that say about the data that HR uses for internal decisions and the reports produced?

Key metrics evaluating organizational performance can be of tremendous significance and useful to decision makers throughout the organization. Jac Fitz-Enz and John R. Mattox II provide a full list of the metrics used to analyze the efficiency, effectiveness, and value of the HR department.[94] This is a valuable book to have on your shelf. When assessing HR performance, they recommend evaluating the following:[95]

- **Efficiency.** Number of open requisitions, positions filled per month, time to fill open positions, salary associated with positions, cost to hire, hires by business unit, amount of training, amount of coaching received, performance improvement plan, job rotation learning path, international assignment, mobile workforce, hours a job requires, cost per job task
- **Effectiveness.** Quality of hire, quality of the recruiting process, quality of service from recruiter, fit with the job, fit with culture, performance rating, high or low potential status, employee engagement, employee loyalty, project management capability, ability to coach, ability to be coached, ability to develop others, ability to create standard procedures
- **Outcomes.** Length of employees' stay, monthly productivity, improved cycle time in job, contributions to customer satisfaction, contributions to quality, increased number of sales, increased margins, improved project quality, improved on-time projects, improved on-budget projects, improved efficiency, increased cost savings, increased innovation, faster product development cycle

Data Analytics and Dashboards

Built into many of the cloud-based talent management systems is the ability to create reports in graphic form. Called a *dashboard,* this feature "displays the current status of metrics and key performance indicators (KPIs) for an organization. Dashboards consolidate and arrange numbers, metrics, and sometimes performance scorecards on a single screen in graphic form."[96] The primary benefit of dashboards is that they provide visual representations of the measures the organization uses to track KPIs. Dashboards also allow the user to generate detailed reports showing new trends, which contribute to the ability to make informed decisions. The dashboard consolidates information from a variety of sources including different systems and databases.[97]

In Chapter 6, there was a case study about m-learning at Fortis Healthcare. Figure 8.1 is a dashboard for that Fortis Healthcare m-learning program. Fortis Healthcare used the following metrics to measure the success of their m-learning sales training program: certification course completion rate, total number of people getting certified for all assigned specialties, and number of application downloads. Examine Figure 8.1 for these measures and how they are displayed. As a standalone system or part of a larger HRS suite, the Learning Management System can provide valuable management information in a variety of formats including dashboards and reports.

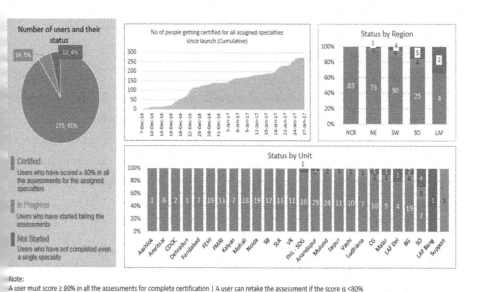

Note:
A user must score ≥ 80% in all the assessments for complete certification | A user can retake the assessment if the score is <80%

Figure 8.1. Fortis Healthcare Sales M-Learning Dashboard

HR SYSTEM TECHNOLOGY TRENDS

In today's 24/7, Internet-driven society, organizations need access to data and information instantaneously. The new HR systems can handle everything involved in the employee life cycle, from onboarding to departure and everything in between. Standard components include recruiting, performance management, training, employee relations, payroll, benefits, time tracking, and scheduling. Unfortunately, many organizations are still bound to the legacy systems they invested in years ago, in some cases at least one system for each of the functions listed above. These systems may contain data in a variety of formats that prevents them from exchanging information. The information in the systems are therefore unreliable and the resulting reports are also unreliable. As businesses move toward holding HR accountable for demonstrating its value, the ability to accurately measure and report HR initiatives becomes of great importance.

The trend in HR systems include reliance upon cloud-enabled suites which integrate major employee life cycle functions and store the data in one place. This then becomes the source of reliable data that can be analyzed and used for decision-making. As mentioned earlier, the new HR technologies can be disruptive because they alter the way HR does business, but they also increase the effectiveness of HR.

Employee Self-Service Portals

The ESS portal enables the employee to access, control, input, and maintain personal information. In so doing, HR offloads some tasks that are time-intensive and frankly less efficient for HR to handle.

Often these functions depend upon an HR system that can be accessed by the employee through an ESS portal. The ESS portal is discussed in more depth in Chapter 11. The relationship to the HR system is that the ESS is a portal that relies upon the information in the HR system(s).

Onboarding

An ESS Portal can be used to provide employees with valuable tools and services, including important information needed during onboarding. Onboarding is the process of orienting and integrating a new employee into an organization. Lin Grensing-Pophal, author of *Human Resource Essentials*, provides us with the elements critical to successful onboarding. Once the hiring decision is made and the offer accepted, it is important to set the scene for what the employee experience will be. The orientation process should do the following: answer questions about items that will specifically impact the new employee, provide a description of the things that affect them as members of their department, and offer an explanation of the things that will impact them as a member of the organization.

Many of these fundamentals can be handled before arrival through online training, forms, and other orientation information available through an ESS portal. Some organizations make this process easier by making the onboarding process—at least when it comes to orientation training—more engaging. Required training can be enhanced by gamification and made accessible through the ESS portal. Wyndham Hotels has an innovative approach to onboarding using gamification as part of its orientation training process, hosted and completion-tracked in the LMS.

· · · · · · · · · · ·
CASE STUDY

Wyndham Hotel Gamification for Onboarding

Annamarie Fairchild

In order to run profitable hotels, owners and general managers of Wyndham properties must maintain high brand standards and properly utilize franchise resources. Wyndham Hotel Group's training department realized that the volume of information can be overwhelming for new owners and managers. They partnered with Designing Digitally Inc. to create an inviting training course that provides an overview of the requirements and available tools.

In the needs analysis process, Designing Digitally Inc. learned that the audience has varying degrees of exposure to the hospitality industry and the Wyndham Hotel Group brand. To accommodate the differing levels of familiarity with hospitality standards and those of Wyndham Hotel, the training allowed new owners and managers to choose the content that they would see. They could omit, or pass by, content they already knew.

After discussing multiple concepts, Wyndham Hotel Group elected to have Designing Digitally Inc. develop a custom website containing traditional e-learning elements. This unique structure allows learners to navigate directly to topics—like they are exploring a website—and yet provides familiar activities such as knowledge checks and narrated videos. Designing Digitally Inc. programmed the website with SCORM reporting so that Wyndham Hotel Group could host it and track learners' completion inside their LMS.

The homepage of the website is a town map. Clicking on a section of the map opens the corresponding training module. The sections animate and the hotel grows as the learner completes modules, indicating that their success is boosting energy throughout the town.

Inside each module, learners move through the scene and click on game cards to launch individual activities. They can unlock enhancements to their fictional property by correctly answering knowledge checks, called Trivia Rounds. The enhancements relate to the scene in which the module takes place, such as new flooring in the hotel lobby or lounge chairs by the pool. After the learner completes the entire course, their hotel has expanded and is brimming with guests.

The illustrated scenes create a realistic hotel setting to which learners can relate. But at the same time, the learning through gamification sets a whimsical, lighthearted tone. Further, the course leaves enough to the imagination to be applicable to any hotel in the Wyndham brand portfolio.

Annmarie Fairweather, Senior Vice President of Global Talent Management for Wyndham Hotel Group, is responsible for collaborating with leadership to assess needs, aggregate and present solutions, and provide strategic direction for talent development, as well as oversee the global design, development, and delivery of learning solutions for all Wyndham Hotel Group associates.

• • • • • • • • • • •

Job Analysis and Position Description

HR systems can also house job analysis, classification, and job descriptions. The jobs are divided into classes based on the level of specific evaluation factors, such as difficulty and variety of work, supervision, originality, nature and purpose of work relationships, experience, and knowledge required. Based on these factors, a grade definition is assigned. This information can be contained in an HR system and made available to employees through the ESS portal.

Time-Tracking and Scheduling Technology

Some HR systems have time-tracking and scheduling capabilities. The task of time tracking—once tedious—has been revolutionized by time-tracking software. All employees enter their own information in the time-tracking system. Easy access to the software on the job facilitates the process. Time tracking can also can be used to track accrued vacation and sick leave. Hours may be reported by individuals or groups and can be made available through the HR system.

Most HR system packages include some kind of tracking for attendance. There are, however, companies that have mastered the science of tracking employee time. Their products can be used as standalone systems or as add-on modules to an HR system. Time-tracking software, similar to the other add-ons mentioned in this chapter, can also be part of a larger ERP system. When the software package is designed specifically for tracking time, regulatory compliance features are often built into the software.

Different industries place varying levels of emphasis on time and attendance. Workers in manufacturing environments may check in and out with time clocks. The HR system software vendors do not provide the hardware, such as clocks, that feed information to the timekeeping software. Timekeeping systems used by the organization will capture the hourly data input by the workers from various time-clock readers throughout a site. That information then has to be downloaded to the HR system, which uses it to arrange employees' schedules. It is also used to gather actual hours worked as well as sick time and vacation time, which is then reviewed before electronic submission to the HR system payroll. Other industries, such as consulting or legal firms, track billed time and utilization levels, and time-tracker software can be customized to that work environment.

Biometrics is an interesting technology that can be used for time tracking. It relies on devices that use an optical reader or a computer chip to identify individuals. Fingerprint scanners use finger geometry to authenticate users. Other biometric technologies include retina scanning, voice recognition, facial scanning, and signature recognition systems. While none of these systems are 100 percent accurate, they can reach very high levels of accuracy.

Performance Management Technology

Performance management (PM) ensures that goals are consistently being met in an effective and efficient manner. Recently, the PM process has changed into an ongoing coaching process, sometimes referred to as "continuous evaluation," rather than the annual, semiannual, or quarterly assessment within the framework of talent management. HR systems with a performance management module streamline the performance management process while maintaining sensitive information in a secure environment. Technology enables ongoing assessment (which is replacing the yearly or biannual performance evaluation). Manager input includes individual performance criteria, measurements to rate performance, and standards for each measure. The entire performance contract is entered into the PM system.

An HR system with a performance management module will allow supervisor and other rater observations, as well as performance incidents, to be input, recorded, tracked, and made available to the employee. There is also space for positive and corrective feedback and recommended development activities. The real value of these data comes from their link to overall corporate goals, a link that is created through the PM system. Using the performance data, the HR system produces summary-level reports. Archived data is necessary in order to track long-term performance trends at both the individual and group levels.

The data can and should be integrated. This involves combining data residing in different sources in order to provide users with a unified view of them. For example, performance and compensation systems may be linked as typically there is a connection between job performance and pay. Merit pay is based on a merit matrix. At the summary level, each employee's data are matched to the matrix and performance dimensions entered in the system. These metrics are used to make decisions about promotions, layoffs, training, and developmental assignments.

The performance management system should also support decision-making. The data important to decision-making include performance criteria, performance measures, performance standards, and performance documentation. These contribute to managers' decision-making. If the performance management system is part of a larger HR system, the system can be programmed to handle different levels of analysis from identifying major performance trends to identifying individual performance issues.

Compensation and Benefits

The link between performance management and compensation as well as other benefits is intuitive, but there must also be a documented link between the performance rating and compensation and the core payroll systems. This can be done through the existing HR system.

While compensation is typically handled in-house and may be part of the HR system, benefit packages are different. Most organizations offer a few different types of benefit programs, including pension or 401(k) plans, workers' compensation or unemployment insurance, long- and short-term disability insurance, and life insurance. Long- and short-term disability insurance both include medical, dental, vision, and other health benefits, and paid time off (PTO). Other benefits sometimes include dependent care; telecommuting, job sharing, or a compressed workweek; employee assistance; and tuition for continuing education. Benefits differ from compensation because employees pay for part of the offering and there is flexibility in these programs. Benefits can be handled by the HR system or benefits can be outsourced.[98]

BUSINESS PROCESS REENGINEERING

Usually, when a new computer system is implemented, it has an impact (sometimes a dramatic one) on business processes. Business process reengineering (BPR) redesigns the work processes to better support the organization's mission and reduce costs. It is a two-phase initiative. Reengineering starts with the organization's mission, strategic goals, and customer needs.

The HR professional asks questions such as, "Does our mission need to be redefined?" "Are our strategic goals aligned with our mission?" and "Who are our customers?" Reengineering often occurs when an HR system is installed.

In this first phase, reengineering concentrates on the organization's current business processes, or the "as-is state." This includes looking at the steps and procedures that govern how resources are used to create products and the services that meet the needs of particular customers or markets.

The second phase is to define the way things will operate in the future (the "to-be state"). In this phase, you develop requirements for the new system. The "to-be state" or future-mode-of-operation (FMO) outlines the functionality desired from the new system, and drives the selection of a new HR system. Define gaps between the current way of doing business and the future way. These are the processes that will need to change. In this phase you also identify any new performance indicators that will be used as a result of the new HR system.

LAWS GOVERNING HR SYSTEM SELECTION

Some of the laws and regulatory agencies that impact the practice of HR in the United States and affect selection of an HR system include the Sarbanes-Oxley Act, the Health Insurance Portability and Accountability Act (HIPAA), the Fair Labor Standards Act (FLSA), the Family and Medical Leave Act (FMLA), the US Civil Rights Act of 1964, Title VII, the Equal Employment Opportunity Commission (EEOC), and the Occupational Safety and Health Administration (OSHA).

Technology can assist with administrating mandated governmental reporting. In fact, an HR system "is essential for accurate, timely record keeping and reporting the facilitates the performance of EEO and OSHA mandates."[99]

There are HR legal organizations, such as Xpert HR and Nolo, that can offer legal services, especially for small and midsized organizations lacking a dedicated legal department. Xpert HR provides comprehensive, state-specific resources that cover all fifty states and the District of Columbia to ensure you stay ahead of the latest legal developments and in line with compliance best practices (http://www.xperthr.com). NoLo is an online resource, endorsed by SHRM, that provides small businesses with legal documents and written legal guidance online (https://store.nolo.com/products/employment-hr).

The good news is that many software and HR system products have compliance standards built into their programs. Additionally, HR management systems can help with regulatory compliance by offering electronic access to data and information. Further, when an organization has an ESS portal, employees have direct access to their benefit information. This empowers employees to maintain the accuracy of their own programs and records. Finally, compliance software systems created for the express purpose of dealing with complex compliance regulations exist and can be added on to HR systems.

In this chapter we examined the HR system in general as well as other standalone systems that handle onboarding, time tracking, scheduling, compensation, benefits, and performance management. We talked about the role of the HR system and its potential impact on business processes. The legal issues and regulatory bodies relevant to the practice of HR in the United States were explained, and we emphasized the fact that HR system must support the goals of the organization and improve organizational performance by capturing, maintaining, and utilizing key metrics.

End-of-Chapter Technology Strategy Questions

Considering your organization's overall business strategy and that of your HR department, as well as the needs of your employees, answer the following:

1. What current challenges does your organization face with regard to talent management and the systems used for such?

2. What reports and data about your organization's employees and HR services inform HR decisions? Are the reports and the systems used reliable or do you question the data and sources?

3. What is the talent management system architecture for your organization? Specifically what system is used to handle each of the HR functions mentioned in this chapter?

Digging Deeper

Dessler, Gary, and Biju Varkkey. 2016. *Human Resource Management.* 14th ed. Noida, IN: Pearson.

Fitz-Enz, Jac, and John R. Mattox II. 2014. *Predictive Analytics for Human Resources.* Hoboken, NJ: Wiley.

Kavanagh, Michael J., Mohan Thite, and Richard D. Johnson. 2015. *Human Resource Information Systems: Basics, Applications, and Future Directions,* 3rd ed. Thousand Oaks, CA: Sage Publishing.

CHAPTER 9

Information Systems Designed for Human Resources

TOPICS COVERED IN THIS CHAPTER

- You know you need an HR system when...

- HR activities and the HR Shared Service Center

- Purpose of information systems designed for HR

- Disruptive technologies and HR systems

- Build, buy, or outsource

- HR system selection

- Game-changing HR systems

- Panasonic goes all-in on Workday

In this chapter, we will use current literature to identify the predominant four different types of HR systems and their functions: HR Information System (HRIS), Talent Management System (TMS), Human Capital Management (HCM) system, and Human Resource Management (HRM) System. The reason you need to know about these systems is because of their effectiveness, flexibility, scalability, accessibility to employee data, analyzing and reporting capabilities, and potential cost effectiveness. Further, an HR system can be configured to work with other standalone systems. So, let's examine these HR systems, realizing that the systems themselves are not the panacea to all HR problems, but they can be of great value to HR in its function as both a shared service center and an HR business partner.

YOU KNOW YOU NEED AN HR SYSTEM WHEN...

When you are confronted with the decision of whether or not your organization should invest in an information system designed specifically for HR functions, the following should provide some clarity. You know your organization needs an HR system when[100]

- Competitiveness in your business sector requires a comprehensive information picture;
- HR relies on data collection and analysis for knowledge and decision-making;
- HR department is mired in details and has no time to contribute on the strategic business level;
- HR department lacks administrative efficiency and effectiveness;
- The role of HR is shifting from transactions to strategic human resource management;
- HR processes and functions are being reengineered;
- The corporate and employee culture demands speedier and more accurate HR services;
- The organization is struggling to recruit; and/or
- Existing, internal legacy systems no longer meet the organization's HR needs.

Figure 9.1. HR System for an SSC
Adapted from Hunter et al., *HR Business Partners*, 34.

Most importantly, if your organization consolidated HR into a shared service center (SSC) model and HR is a trusted business partner, you are ready for a HR system that is designed specifically for HR functions. Those functions include hiring, performance management, training, employee relations, payroll, benefits, pensions, and departures (see Figure 9.1).[101]

HR ACTIVITIES AND THE HR SHARED SERVICE CENTER

Technology has evolved and matured over the past ten to twenty years. Newer HR systems typically are cloud-based and therefore capitalize on current technology trends, including data analytics, mobile access, social media, and IoT. While HR systems have been evolving, HR roles and activities have changed in many ways as well. Nevertheless, typical HR functions remain intact. Kavanagh, Thite, and Johnson sort twentieth-century HR activities into three broad categories:[102]

- **Transactional** activities include day-to-day transactions involving recordkeeping, such as payroll info, employee status changes, and employee benefit administration.

- **Traditional** activities include programs such as planning, recruiting, selection, training, compensation, and performance management.
- **Transformational** activities are those that add value through cultural or organizational change, strategy, innovation, or realignment.

The same authors comment that in the past, most HR professionals spent about 65–75 percent of their time on transactional, 15–30 percent of their time on traditional activities, and 5–15 percent of their time on transformational activities.[103]

With the advent of new and powerful HR systems that incorporate AI, social media, data analytics, mobile computing, and cloud computing, HR departmental responsibilities shifted and so did the competencies required of HR professionals. Using the terminology of Kavanagh, Thite, and Johnson, the majority of current HR functions have evolved into transformational activities. In fact, David Ulrich, a leading thinker on HR contributions to organizations, makes the following bold statement: "HR department activities, rather than individual HR talent, have predominant impact on business performance and stakeholder value."[104] He emphasizes that HR must add value by affecting organizational change, contributing to the business strategy, providing innovative and creative solutions, and realigning business practices to meet the new business culture and technology needs. This is a lot of responsibility placed on HR. That said, HR-specific systems and other technologies can assist the HR profession in performing its new, more sophisticated, challenging functions. Using information systems designed specifically for HR, the effectiveness, power, and influence of the HR department can increase exponentially.

PURPOSE OF INFORMATION SYSTEMS DESIGNED FOR HR

Much of the HR literature refers to the information systems designed for HR as Human Resource Information Systems (HRIS), clustering all systems used by HR into that category. The term HRIS has been around for a couple decades. Kavanagh, Thite, and Johnson define an HRIS in general terms as "a system used to acquire, store, manipulate, analyze, retrieve, and distribute information regarding an organization's human resources to support HR and managerial decisions."[105]As such, an HRIS could pertain to any number of systems that all fall into that category of systems that manage HR-related information. In the last five years, the HRIS offerings have become more powerful, complex, and multifaceted with different levels of sophistication.

What follows is a typology of HR systems in table form summarizing general HR systems, their names, and the HR functions performed by systems of that type (Table 9.1). *Note:* There will be exceptions where vendors

Table 9.1. HR Systems Typology

Core Components	HRIS	TMS	HCM	HRM
Recruiting/Applicant Tracking System	X	X	X	X
Benefits Administration	X	X	X	X
Absence Management	X	X	X	X
Compensation Management	X	X	X	X
Training and Development	X	X	X	X
Workflow	X	X	X	X
Self-Service	X	X	X	X
Reporting	X	X	X	X
Career Planning		X	X	X
Succession Planning		X	X	X
Performance Management		X	X	X
Learning Management		X	X	X
Workforce Planning			X	X
Competency Management			X	X
Performance Planning			X	X
Compensation Planning			X	X
Time and Expense Management			X	X
Hiring			X	X
Onboarding			X	X
Contingent Workforce Management			X	X
Organization Visualization			X	X
Complex Predictive Analytics			X	X
Complex Workflow			X	X
Payroll				X
Time & Labor				X

add other functions to the suite of offerings for any given HR system type. This table is not a definitive list of system types and functions; rather, it is meant to provide general guidance and give some structure to categories of HR systems.

Many organizations have a variety of HR legacy systems that do not use cloud computing. The trend is to move toward a consumption-based operations and pricing model. This means that pricing varies based upon the services used, a fundamental attribute of cloud computing. The truth is, cloud-based HR systems are powerful.

Current HR system offerings are cloud based, whether an HRIS, talent management system, HCM system, or Human Resource Management System (HRMS). Hunter et al. point out how important it is to use an HR system. It serves as the basis for implementing an HRBP model (HR Business Partner mentioned in Chapter 2).[106] The HRBP model relies on a Shared Service Center (SSC) to provide HR customer service to business partners and employees (the customer). This approach is modeled after other functional areas such as IT, finance, and procurement.

Shared Service Center benefits include driving down administrative overhead costs (through streamlining administrative tasks), creating a relationship between costs and service, improving service quality, and maximizing technology investments primarily by consolidating systems and eliminating system redundancies.[107] The HR system gives the HR Business Partner a *single version of truth,* which means that there is a centralized database that contains the fully aligned, clean, and reliable data.[108]

DISRUPTIVE TECHNOLOGIES AND HR SYSTEMS

The HR systems field is experiencing a cataclysmic change. Josh Bersin speaks to this very issue and the changing landscape of HR systems providers: "Instability is being driven by the shift from cloud to mobile; the explosion in analytics and artificial intelligence; and the emergence of video, social recruiting, and wearables in the workplace. Everything is changing, and quickly—including the types of technology HR professionals use, the experiences those systems deliver, and the underlying software designs—making many of the traditional HR systems purchased only a decade ago seem out of date."[109]

How do these technology trends impact HR practice? Essentially, they primarily affect the areas of performance management, people analytics, learning, talent acquisition, team management, health and wellness, and automated HR. Let's examine a few of these. We have already discussed how learning environments are replacing traditional learning programs and how cloud, social, and mobile technologies impact learning. What has changed regarding the other functions? Here are some of the bigger changes:

- **Performance management**—which was a soft skill and qualitative process—is now data-driven, assessed through pulse surveys that are distributed directly to mobile devices using integrated directories, enhanced by gamification features, and conducted continuously, enabled by cloud computing.
- **People analytics** (or **workforce analytics**) use modeling software to obtain predictive analytics for job progression and career next step established through networks recognized through an analysis of email patterns.
- **Talent acquisition** that is propelled by mobile and cloud-based software can handle end-to-end recruitment and record all of the qualified candidates in an applicant tracking system.
- **Team management**, which is integrated into the HR system, enabled through the cloud, and delivered to the mobile device, provides collaboration, project management, and workflow management tools that were previously only the domain of the organization's divisions outside HR.
- **Automated HR** has been rocked by the incorporation of AI in the fiber of the program, such that AI advisement is a natural feature of the cloud-based HR system on topics including guidance on career, learning, and leadership decisions at the individual level.

All of these functions can be supported by an HR system.

BUILD, BUY, OR OUTSOURCE

Not every organization can afford to eliminate existing legacy systems and replace them with an HR system. Luckily, there are options. Three basic choices are involved in the physical design of the HR system: you can build your own organization-specific HR system, find a commercial off-the-shelf (COTS) system, or outsource the function, letting another organization handle it. All three choices impact costs to varying degrees. In the three approaches, four different elements should influence the final decision on acquisition strategy: the business need, in-house skills, project management skills, and timeframe.

Build

When the business need is unique and the in-house skills exist both at the functional and technical level, then building the system in-house is an attractive option. There should be a skilled in-house project manager. The development timeframe can be flexible if using in-house or external developers. The advantages include customization and control over all aspects of the development. The software is guaranteed to meet the business requirements, and there will be increased flexibility and innovative solutions for accommodating business processes.

Commercial Off-the-Shelf

A COTS system is appropriate when the business need is considered standard. COTS is a prepackaged commercial product that has been tested and is stable. It can be purchased and configured to meet the business needs. There will, no doubt, need to be modifications made to accommodate internal business processes.

Outsource

Outsourcing the function allows you to leverage another organization's system and processes. Outsourcing has its advantages. Often HR departments outsource payroll. In that case, the vendor may have both the system and the processes.

HR SYSTEM SELECTION

The impact of cloud computing can be seen dramatically when talking about HR system selection. Traditionally, this decision was made based on the answers to basic technology and cost questions. Those have now been replaced by a focus on function. While these questions are still important, due diligence has shifted to an analysis of what major HR functions the organization needs performed by a system. However, cost does still impact selection. Compiling requirements and budget leads to analysis of vendors who offer systems satisfying both. The basic steps of HR system selection remain the same, but they are not as detailed: [110]

1. Know what you want the system to do (system requirements).
2. Know your audience and their needs.
3. Research what peers are saying about best-in-class vendors.
4. Develop a Request for Proposal (RFP) to vet potential vendors and invite the top three or four RFP respondents to demonstrate their capabilities.
5. Do your homework by getting the vendor's references and following up on them, and then make a selection.
6. Close the deal, but be prepared to negotiate.

GAME-CHANGING HR SYSTEMS

Organizations adopting a new HR system find that business processes are impacted and will need to be revised. Additionally, the technology system architecture will most certainly change. Here is the good news: Investment in an HR system may change the business processes, but it also offers advantages. Scalable implementation of cloud-based HR systems can offer savings— pay for what is used and no more. Additionally, cloud HR technologies are leading edge, typically incorporating mobile, social, big data analytics, and IoT. This offers obvious benefits to larger organizations but also enables small and medium-size organizations to have a technological online presence that is sophisticated and leading edge. [111]

Cloud computing offers scalable, agile, and distributable capabilities that enable smaller organizations to reach optimum performance immediately by lifting and shifting selected functions to the cloud. Further, as the organization grows, other functions can be added. Since you pay for what you use and don't pay for functions you don't use, the savings accumulate. This is the benefit of being asset light, or not investing in the equipment.

The HR system can be approached in a modular fashion allowing for economies of scale. Identify the HR software features that are required at present and add other features later as needs change. This is the recipe for success and truly unique to the new cloud-enabled HR technologies. Couple that with a digital mindset and the result is an agile HR department.

CASE STUDY

Panasonic Goes All-In on Workday

Joe Calcaterra and Allegra Kipnis

In 2011, Panasonic's HR team was looking for an HCMS that could deliver efficiency improvements and smooth the process of managing an international talent base. They needed something scalable that was sensitive to the changing consumer technologies that were creating new employee expectations for self-service in real-time for many functions. It was clear that mobile was the developing frontier for this kind of customer experience, with smartphones taking over the consumer technology world. The internal HR information services team needed a scalable, globally accessible, and eventually mobile solution to support its changing business.

From 1997 to 2011, Panasonic's "legacy" system had delivered good results, but it was limited to domestic functionality and could not easily be scaled or integrated with other software or systems. Looking to the future, HR needed a global view of employees and a way to continue adding services and functionality. Upgrading the legacy system was simply too costly and required too many technical resources. After careful consideration, Panasonic decided to migrate to the Workday platform, embracing the cloud and all its flexibility.

HR leadership sat down to determine where they needed to improve, and agreed that efficiency and consistency topped the list. They also looked at their roadmap and realized that as Panasonic moved forward, the ability to integrate new functionality and future vendor services into the HCMS would be key to improving the end-user experience while streamlining workflow at the HR level. The goals were simple: eliminate redundancy, minimize errors, and deliver a great customer experience to employees around the world. Soon, functionality for performance reviews, time tracking, and absence management became entrenched in Workday, and manager feedback became more consistent and far easier for employees to understand and access. The switch was paying off!

Another area that got a boost was real-time feedback. Workday's customizable KPI worklet functionality allows managers across the company access to the dashboards and data that guide daily decisions. In HR, the recruiting team members access their KPI worklet to review HR analytics such as quality of hire and time to fill positions. For senior management, the worklet provides greater transparency into the makeup of the workforce—it's data driving diversity as leaders can factor that into hiring and promotions. This single source of information reduced the need for additional programs and training, and further integrated Workday usage into the fabric of daily life at Panasonic.

Beyond HR's goals, the transition to Workday has yielded benefits unanticipated in 2011. At the time, smartphone usage was catching on, and mobile apps were still in their infancy when it came to corporate-level security or complex functionality. Over the last few years, growth in mobile technology has allowed Panasonic to leverage an incredible strength of the Workday system: remote access. Workday does not require an intranet connection. It can be accessed from any web browser just by logging in, and there is an app for most smartphones. End users can self-serve many common HR functions, and can even print key documents like W-2s or paystubs right from their mobile devices. While this may sound like a nice-to-have, Panasonic has acquired major industrial businesses between 2015 and 2017, onboarding more than four thousand employees who do not utilize company email or receive company electronics. Important email communications like benefits changes or compensation updates can be pushed to these employees via the Workday portal and accessed on mobile device or web browser, reducing the gap in the employee's HR experience between office positions and production positions.

With Workday, HR at Panasonic is driving user engagement, enjoying huge efficiency improvements, offering new digital programs through the platform, and staying future forward every day.

Joe Calcaterra, Director of HR Services and head of the HRIS Team, has been with Panasonic for over twenty years. His expertise in both HR and IT functional areas makes him an effective and inspiring leader within the HR organization.

Allegra Kipnis, Internal Communications Specialist, is a communications and marketing professional with a focus on culture and development. She joined Panasonic in 2017 to help focus communications on building connections between employees and the company.

· · · · · · · · · · · ·

HR systems vary in size, sophistication, and functionality. There are a variety of features offered by these HR systems, so selection of an HR system should be based on what the particular organization needs it to do.

It is unlikely that your organization will choose to get rid of all of its present systems. You may find that your organization has existing legacy HR systems that still perform well. In such cases an integration with a larger HR system or gradual phase out of the legacy system may be the answer. The system architecture will vary based on our organization's specific needs, HR Technology Strategy, and existing HR systems. Always rely on and collaborate with your IT professionals in-house when it comes to the system architecture. Typically, organizations build/buy/outsource a hybrid of standalone systems (for timekeeping or benefits for instance) that can work with the chosen HR system. As mentioned in the introduction, experts agree (at the time of this writing) that there is no single system that handles all HR functions well. Each system, no matter how sophisticated, has functions that are not as robust as a standalone comparable. So be prepared for this hybrid possibility.

Collaboration with your HR Business Partners is key in the HR system selection process. Although the system primarily handles HR functions, many departments will be impacted by it, so representatives from other functional areas should participate in the selection and implementation of the

HR system. And of course you should always work hand in hand with the IT department.

End-of-Chapter HR Technology Strategy Questions

Considering your organization's overall business strategy and that of your HR department, as well as the needs of your employees, answer the following:

1. Take an inventory of the systems used to perform HR functions—hiring, performance management, training, employee relations, payroll, benefits, pensions, and departures. (If you can get an HR system architecture from the IT department, that is even better!) What requirements does your organization have for an HR system that are not being met by the current HR system technology architecture?
2. What additional HR functions offered by an HR system or by integrated, standalone systems (e.g., e-recruiting, payroll, time keeping, etc.) would benefit your organization and why?
3. How would an HR system optimize the overall HR technology strategy and align with the organizational strategy?
4. How should your organization prepare for the changes of an HR system?

Digging Deeper

Harvard Business Review. 2011. *HBR's 10 Must Reads on Change Management.* Boston, MA: Harvard Business Review Press.

Hunter, Ian, Jane Saunders, Allan Boroughs, and Simon Constance. 2016. *HR Business Partners.* 2nd ed. New York: Routledge.

Kavanagh, Michael J., Mohan Thite, and Richard D. Johnson. 2015. *Human Resource Information Systems: Basics, Applications, and Future Directions.* 3rd ed. Thousand Oaks, CA: Sage Publishing.

Ulrich, Dave, David Kryscynski, Mike Ulrich, and Wayne Brockbank. 2017. *Victory through Organization: Why the War for Talent Is Failing Your Company and What You Can Do about It.* New York: McGraw-Hill.

CHAPTER 10

E-recruiting

TOPICS COVERED IN THIS CHAPTER

- E-recruiting trends

- Twenty-first-century recruiting basics

- E-recruiting benefits and pitfalls

- Cloud computing's impact on e-recruiting

- Applicant tracking systems

- Big data, analytics, and predictive analytics

- Security

- Legal considerations

- Carilion Clinic: e-recruitment and the shortage of nurses

In the twenty-first century, a new breed of online recruiting seized the recruiting niche of corporate jobsite hosting. Instead of handling the complex hiring process as a face-to-face endeavor, organizations use online, cloud-based solutions to streamline the recruitment process. This is called *e-recruiting* because it allows users to handle the recruitment process online. These e-recruiting systems could either be standalone or incorporated in a larger HR system as demonstrated in the Table 9.1.

Another change occurred concurrently: While in the twentieth century, "assets" referred to the cash and physical property a company owned, organizations now tout their employees as their greatest "assets"—thus the emergence of the phrase "human capital." This shift is important because organizations now focus more on hiring and keeping their employees; the success of an organization in part depends upon hiring the right people. Consequently, the quality of recruits and new hires receives much importance and attention, and recruiting has emerged as a very important HR function. How does an organization attract quality people and hire them? Today's HR executives and recruiters are asking questions like the following:

- How many and what sort of worker do we need to succeed and move forward?
- What challenges present themselves as we compete for this talent?
- How will we address potential shortages of people and skills in the available talent pool?
- How will we preserve and enhance the culture and values of the organization?
- What measures can we take to identify and retain effective strategic leaders for the future?

Answers to these questions frame the e-recruiting strategy that drives consideration of which tools to use for recruiting.

In this chapter, we will address recruiting head on. We will examine current e-recruiting trends, how those have impacted the approach to e-recruiting, and the role emerging technologies should play. With regard to practical application of these concepts, the case study demonstrates how an e-recruiting strategy coupled with innovative use of technology reversed the nursing shortage at one hospital.

E-RECRUITING TRENDS

E-recruiting allows the host organization to perform all of the computer-based actions (which are usually cloud enabled) related to recruitment. From the comfort of their computers, users can create a library of job requisitions, establish those requisitions, post to more than one thousand job boards, and use a centralized database of candidates for searching and managing applicant information with an ATS. The most significant departure from twentieth-century recruiting is the inclusion of social media, cloud computing, IoT, data analytics, and mobile devices in the recruiting strategy. In combination, these technologies make the recruiting process more user friendly, faster, (potentially) cheaper, and more strategic. No aspect of HR better demonstrates the impact of these disruptive technologies than recruiting.

Twenty-First-Century Recruiting Basics

The recruiting process involves the following steps. Typically, the first step is to identify a vacancy, then develop a position description. Developing a recruitment plan is followed by selecting a search committee. The next step is to post the position and implement the recruitment plan. Review applications to create a shortlist of possible candidates. Conduct interviews and make a selection. Make the offer, and if it is accepted the conditions of hire are finalized. While these steps are standard, the process of performing these steps has changed. That is because much of it can be done automatically.

Some hiring metrics for evaluating the effectiveness of internal hiring processes include measuring

- Diversity and inclusion,
- Candidate experience,
- Quality of hire,
- Cost of hire,
- Time to hire, and
- Overall recruiting process efficiency.

The attraction of metrics is really a result of the big data and data analytics phenomena and the desire to use data to inform the decision-making process.[112]

E-RECRUITING BENEFITS AND PITFALLS

Like any other process, e-recruiting has both positives and negatives. The primary advantage is its significant cost savings: companies have reported savings of 95 percent when changing from traditional to online recruiting sources, especially ones that are cloud-enabled. Other benefits of e-recruiting include higher applicant response-rate; software that can be used to weed out unqualified applicants; applicant data that are easily searched by using keywords, job histories, and other relevant items; and efficiencies that can shorten the recruitment cycle. Now that IoT is also built into many of the e-recruiting cloud-based systems, the process is even more streamlined. IoT has created access to volumes of information, providing more data that can be analyzed and interpreted in the recruiting process.[113]

On the flip side, there are negative aspects to e-recruiting. Poor website design can harm recruitment outcomes. If the navigation and user interface are poorly conceived, jobseekers may not be attracted to the site. Poor design also reflects negatively on the organization, thereby potentially diminishing the appeal to high-caliber applicants. Further, if the website does not accurately represent the organization, an applicant's disappointment may impact their satisfaction, performance, commitment, job involvement, and tenure once she is hired.

CLOUD COMPUTING'S IMPACT ON E-RECRUITING

White papers and articles on the topic of cloud computing and recruiting abound. One attractive asset is the scalability of cloud-based e-recruiting. You only pay for what you use. The service is fully managed by the provider. The consumer/applicant needs nothing but a personal computer or a mobile device. The cloud extends the reach of e-recruiting and sourcing capabilities such that possible candidates can be sourced from anywhere in the world. This becomes important in job categories where the pool of qualified applicants may be limited.

Mobile Recruiting

Access to recruiting sites from a mobile device is not just commonplace; it is now expected. Thus, any organization developing a recruiting strategy should have a mobile component to that strategy. As the smartphone becomes an ever more integral part of society, recruitment is also modified by the technology. Employers who want to attract qualified talent need to ensure that online job advertising and application processes are seamless, convenient, and optimized for mobile devices. The need for mobile-friendly recruiting is particularly evident in the aspects of recruiting related to attracting and retaining talent. This is not an age-specific requirement: a study done by Michael Lawson for a local government in Aurora, Colorado, indicates that all generations prefer mobile-friendly job websites.[114]

Social Networks and Recruiting

Social media can be used for every aspect of recruitment, from sourcing, attraction, application, and selection, to onboarding (where the new hire connects with other employees) and during employment.[115] When integrating social media in the recruitment strategy, HR must work very closely with IT to implement the strategy within the parameters of the existing technology infrastructure. HR must also collaborate with the organization's marketing group, as the presentation of social recruiting pertains to branding, a marketing domain.

One of the most effective uses of social media can be preemptively finding qualified candidates. This process is called *sourcing* and it is the primary use of social media that we will examine here. Sourcing is "the proactive identification, engagement, and assessment of talent focusing solely on non-applicants with the end goal of producing qualified, interested, and available candidates."[116] Sourcing can be done on social networks such as LinkedIn, the world's largest online professional network. A basic LinkedIn account is free and represents the most cost-effective solution for small organizations. Searching for new, qualified talent in LinkedIn can be done through simple keyword searches. Potential candidates can be contacted within the platform using the "connect" and "messaging" features. Joining LinkedIn groups can be used to enlarge the client base. On an individual level, a follow-up via messaging and a request for email can secure an introduction. A great text that fully examines use of social media and social networking for recruiting purposes is Andy Headworth's *Social Media Recruitment* (2015), which is listed under the "Digging Deeper" section.

Here is where marketing comes in. Once potential hires are contacted, it is likely they will look up your organization. It is important to have a clear profile of your organization on your website. This branding can either attract or repel your candidates.

TIPS AND TOOLS FOR E-RECRUITING

- Be aware of the metrics used for HR functions and use them.
- Rely on more than one sourcing method for recruiting.
- Pay attention to the company website and branding to ensure it is up-to-date and attractive.
- Ensure that you have an effective ATS, especially to record applicants who were final candidates.
- Determine whether your e-recruiting software should be part of a larger HR system, outsourced, or standalone, but integrated with an HR system.
- Make your recruiting process mobile friendly.

APPLICANT TRACKING SYSTEMS

An ATS is "a software application designed to help an enterprise recruit employees more efficiently. It can be used to post job openings on a corporate website or job board, screen résumés, and generate interview requests to potential candidates by email. Other features may include individual applicant tracking, requisition tracking, automated résumé ranking, customized input forms, prescreening questions and response tracking, and multilingual capabilities."[117]

Features of a standard ATS include integration capabilities with other systems, social network recruiting, job board integration, analytics, inclusion in talent acquisition suites, and increased automation,[118] but the most valuable aspect of the ATS is its follow-up capabilities. Having a record of all vetted candidates can shorten the hiring process. For instance, if a second opening should occur for the same job type, or the candidate to whom an offer was tendered turns down the offer, then previously vetted candidates in the applicant pool could be considered. Thus, ATS can cut costs.

BIG DATA, ANALYTICS, AND PREDICTIVE ANALYTICS FOR RECRUITING

Metrics are used to quantify the cost and impact of employee programs as well as to measure the success of HR initiatives. *Analytics* is the process of combining data mining with business analytics techniques to analyze the resulting data using the metrics as the categories worthy of analysis. The goal of human resource analytics is to unearth insights that inform how we manage employees to reach business goals. Analytics, when used correctly, can also be predictive.

Predictive analytics use metrics combined with employee turnover data to provide insights into turnover and how to prevent it. The result is that you can "predict" which candidates will be high performers. This information enables you to hire the right people from the start. You can also use predictive analytics to identify high performers who may be at risk of leaving the organization and intervene before that happens.

SECURITY

The concern about the security of personal information on e-recruiting websites and services is ongoing and real. Should the systems be hacked to unlock a lot of private data, much is at risk. Social networks are especially vulnerable since little vetting of members is performed other than the members' right to block individuals or organizations, and most are hosted in the public cloud. Standard IT security solutions should be invoked and monitored.

LEGAL CONSIDERATIONS

Regulations abound regarding how to solicit and handle applicant information. US laws dictate that employers maintain detailed information about applicants. Technology can assist in this area by using an ATS. But the quantity and quality of applicants is heavily dependent upon the screening that occurs during the e-recruiting process.

E-recruiting technology can be configured to accommodate and abide by the laws of different countries. However, the job descriptions posted are typically written by humans and humans can make mistakes. Of particular importance is the avoidance of terms in the job description that may demonstrate employment discrimination against a race, community, disability, lifestyle, or age group.

It is important to be aware of employment laws. A good source that addresses the interface of recruiting and legal issues is Nolo (https://www.nolo.com). However, some basics include the following:[119]

- Ensure your website is accessible to the visually impaired.
- Avoid intentional screening of protected groups.
- Use e-recruiting for jobs requiring computer skills; if they are not required, consider low-tech alternatives.

Follow the Internet Applicant Rule as stated by the Department of Labor: "The Internet Applicant rule addresses recordkeeping by Federal contractors and subcontractors about the Internet hiring process and the solicitation of race, gender, and ethnicity of 'Internet Applicants.'"[120]

Online selection processes should be mapped to these criteria in order to be compliant with US federal law. Although many seekers may approach the job website, only the truly qualified should become applicants. In order to avoid diluting the pool of qualified applicants with those who are unqualified, follow the preceding guidelines. One highly successful e-recruiting strategy is exemplified below in the Carilion Clinic Case.

• • • • • • • • • • •
CASE STUDY

Carilion Clinic: E-recruitment and the Shortage of Nurses

Susan Swayze, PhD, MBA, and Johanna Sweet, EdD, MBA

The nursing labor shortage is a major challenge for hospitals. Recruiters must be creative and intentional in their recruitment efforts to attract and hire qualified registered nurses (RNs)—especially millennials in search of organizations that provide meaningful career experiences. In order to fill positions where demand far outpaces supply, recruiting outside one's geographic area is typically a necessity. For one hospital, Carilion Clinic, the skillful use of e-recruitment has enabled the organization to hire qualified candidates for hard to fill positions in the competitive healthcare environment.

With thirteen thousand employees, Carilion is the largest employer in the Roanoke, Virginia, metropolitan area. Carilion is an academic teaching institution comprising seven hospitals in both urban and rural areas. Carilion receives on average fifty thousand applications each year, with fifteen recruiters filling more than four thousand positions annually—of these, 60 percent are hired externally. Carilion recognizes that in order to increase the pool of qualified candidates, e-recruitment is the most strategic way to connect with both passive and active candidates. Like most organizations, when a position becomes open, the position description is immediately posted to the company website as well as to position-specific external job websites. To increase applications for hard-to-fill positions, Carilion also posts the position descriptions on Indeed, Facebook, LinkedIn, and Glassdoor to increase exposure to potential applicants.

Carilion's use of Glassdoor has been particularly fruitful. Through the inclusion of content that provides an insider's view of the organization, Carilion experienced a 97 percent increase in page view traffic in one year (from 3,652 to 6,662 monthly views). Carilion pays particular attention to keywords in the position announcement so that in a Google search, a link to their job postings will be at the top of the search feed. Additionally, Carilion effectively uses geofencing—online ads targeting specific groups in a virtual geographic boundary—to promote their hospital and open positions. Through e-recruiting, Carillion has maintained a time-to-fill metric of less than sixty-five days while experiencing an increase in hard-to-fill positions.

Carilion Clinic also acknowledges that a key success factor in nurse recruitment is to make the process convenient for the candidate and to streamline the "interest to interview" process. Carilion does not wait for a completed application for nursing positions; they schedule an interview with an interested candidate based on their résumé and gather the completed application later. This streamlined process is necessary in a competitive landscape where demand for qualified nurses far exceeds supply. A qualified nurse can be recruited away from an organization in the time it takes to complete and review an application.

"Live chat" has allowed Carilion to tailor the application experience to the nurse candidate, while streamlining the hiring process. Carilion utilized a free, Internet-based application to create their live chat capability and created a strategy for live chat availability based on data analytics that showed peak search times for nursing positions. When a person clicks on the live chat icon, the recruiter is alerted to begin an interaction. Through live chat, an interested nurse can speak to a recruiter within seconds. Live chat allows the drag and drop of résumés so that recruiters can gather immediate information and begin the application process. One example: An RN called into live chat from West Virginia and had an interview scheduled with the hiring manager within twenty minutes of the live chat start time. In the past year, Carilion has participated in one thousand live chat sessions. In this time period, nurse hires have increased by 9 percent, and a new hiring record has been set.

Every year it takes more and more effort to fill open nursing positions. Carilion's approach to recruitment is similar to many organizations in the use of social media to advertise hard-to-fill positions, but differs in the interest to interview process that their nurse candidates experience. By utilizing various e-recruitment techniques, Carilion has created an advantage in filling nursing positions in the competitive healthcare environment.

Susan Swayze, PhD, MBA, is an Associate Professor of Educational Research at The George Washington University and an organizational development consultant.

Johanna Sweet, MBA, EdD, is an Assistant Professor of Business Administration and Economics at The George Washington University.

• • • • • • • • • •

In this chapter, we discussed the pros and cons of e-recruiting. We examined the impact of disruptive technologies on e-recruiting. The variety of options available for implementing e-recruiting were highlighted. We emphasized the fact that e-recruiting can be a module within an HR systems or a stand-alone software that is part of the overall system architecture. It can even be outsourced. Finally, we addressed the legal considerations associated with e-recruiting.

End-of-Chapter Technology Strategy Questions

Considering your organization's HR technology strategy, as well as the needs of your employees, answer the following:

1. How does e-recruiting align with your organization's HR technology strategy?
2. To what extent has your organization embraced data analytics and how is it being used to increase the effectiveness of your organization's recruiting approach?
3. What types of change would need to occur in your organization's existing recruiting approach in order to accommodate e-recruiting?
4. Going forward, what recruiting data will be most relevant and important for your organization to gather and why?

Digging Deeper

Davenport, Thomas H., Jeanne Harris, and Jeremy Shapiro. 2010. "Competing on Talent Analytics." *Harvard Business Review* 88 (10): 52–58.

Grensing-Pophal, Lin. 2010. *Human Resource Essentials: Your Guide to Starting and Running the HR Function.* 2nd ed. Alexandria, VA: Society for Human Resource Management.

Headworth, Andy. 2015. *Social Media Recruitment: How to Successfully Integrate Social Media into Recruitment Strategy.* Philadelphia: KoganPage.

Isson, Jean Paul, and Jesse S. Harriott. 2016. *People Analytics in the Era of Big Data: Changing the Way You Attract, Acquire, Develop, and Retain Talent.* Hoboken, NJ: John Wiley and Sons. Particularly pages 131–203.

Meister, Jeanne C., and Kevin J. Mulcahy. 2017. *The Future Workplace Experience: 10 Rules for Mastering Disruption in Recruiting and Engaging Employees*. New York: McGraw Hill Education.

CHAPTER 11

The Powerful Human Resource Portal

TOPICS COVERED IN THIS CHAPTER

- What is a portal?

- Portal design

- The HR professional and HR portals

- Employee self-service portals

- Mobile portals

Portals are powerful tools that serve as entryways to organizations; they can be visible to customers and potential clients or offer points of access for employees to use in-house services. The portal can be particularly useful to HR and our customers, the employees. A portal works well with an HR system, providing employees with access to their personal information, training, job openings, and benefits. For the HR department, the portal displays the latest HR news, policy changes, surveys, resource information, and the like. A well-designed portal attracts users; a poorly designed portal does not. Consequently, basic portal design principles appear in this chapter. In lieu of a case study, two versions of the same portal are examined—one for PC and the other for mobile access—for design implications.

WHAT IS A PORTAL?

A *web portal* is a site on the Internet that typically offers personalized capabilities to its visitors, providing a doorway to other content. It is both the entrance and the kiosk of capabilities for a large corporation. It is usually the first thing the visitor sees, and as we know, first impressions really count. Portals should be designed to accommodate both PC and mobile access.

Organizations that invest in a portal are generally deliberate in taking full advantage of its features. The power of the portal is in the variety of tools, services, information, search features, and communication venues it offers. Using a portal as nothing more than a website is like attaching a racehorse to a plow: you will not realize its full potential. Portals, like racehorses, are made for high performance. So why not use all of the portal's capacity if you decided to invest in one?

To achieve the optimal use of your portal, design is all-important. Portals are only as good as the content and services they offer. If the information isn't valuable to the visitors, the portal will fail. To grab the user's attention, be sure to focus on business processes. Dan Sullivan, author of *The Proven Portal*, emphasizes that portals should be designed to solve a problem that relates to an important business operation, such as customer service or managing human resource functions.

As mentioned above, there are external and internal portals. Let's examine generic design elements for both. Then we will look specifically at the ESS portal, most commonly used by HR.

PORTAL DESIGN

A powerful portal should incorporate ease of use, personalization, online decision support, useful functions (which differs from ease-of-use), a search feature, RSS, single point of access, and social media. Each is described further below. Keep the visual element in mind as well. While there is a lot of real estate to cover on the portal page, not every inch should be filled. Grouping similar information and functions can streamline the look and feel. The last thing you want is a confusing appearance.

Ease of Use

The attributes of the portal must be evident and navigation should be intuitive. If it is unnecessarily complicated, you will drive away users. Be sure that the portal is designed from the user's perspective. For example, the *single-sign-on* environment is attractive because it reduces the number of passwords users have to remember. Users sign on using one login and password and then can have access to a variety of services. Many organizations now combine single sign on (SSO) with multifactor identification (which adds a set of two or more unique identifiers to authenticate the individual).

Personalization

Portals allow users to customize their settings in a way that fits personal preferences and interests. Personalization can include anything from a custom start-up page, a custom directory, or automatic notification of new content. This is especially important for portals that users frequently visit. Workplace portals for HR functions, for example, can be customized so that the functions used most often are highlighted by and visible in the portal.

Online Decision Support

Decision-support tools (such as for PM) are designed to help employees gather information to make an evaluation or judgment, such as comparing or calculating something. In the case of PM, the HR system offers access to all of the information necessary to make performance decisions—including performance criteria, performance measures, performance standards, goal-setting results, and recent performance documentation—in a single place.[121] Some say that online decision support is equivalent to having a personal consultant because it guides you through the process of making a choice. For HR professionals, these decision-support features in an HR portal significantly reduce the time spent on administrative tasks that can be handled by the employees themselves.

Useful Functions

Be sure the portal provides access to multiple systems; it should not be the front end of one system. If this is the case, the portal is underused. Provide access to functions that people want. If product comparisons are part of what your organization offers (in, for example, a travel portal), then make that easily accessible. How will you know which functions are most valuable to the users? That is where big data and data analytics become important. Your IT department can provide tracking information that tells you which aspect of the portal is "hit" most frequently.

Search Feature

A powerful search feature in the portal will increase its attractiveness. Search tools should work across multiple systems. Further, through the practice known as enterprise search, search vendors now can create tools that index documents and other texts from intranets, document management systems, email folders, and database applications. As the portal's search capabilities increase, so does the likelihood that the portal will be used.

RSS Feeds

One feature that many portals incorporate is the RSS feed. RSS is a family of web feed formats used to publish frequently updated digital content. RSS feeds allow users to be notified of new content without having to actively check for it. The advantage of an RSS feed for portals is that it can be used behind firewalls. It provides information such as news updates, stock prices, weather, and commodities. You can also receive podcasts. The RSS feeds can be customized to your business.

Single Point of Access

The HR portal is the entryway to all of the offices needed for HR functions. It displays a wide spectrum of information, from corporate data to HR resources, travel arrangements, expense filing, internal purchasing, researching, and a myriad of other tools and information. The single point of access offers self-service with ease. For internal HR portals, the customer/user is the employee. Internal portals should combine customer profiling and intelligent content technology to encourage return visits.

For an example of a portal that accomplishes many of these objectives, see the internal portal for George Washington University employees and students (Figure 11.1). Students with access to this portal can essentially handle everything related to beginning and completing a degree without ever needing to step foot on the campus, meaning that a degree can be earned from anywhere in the world. Online degree programs typically have a portal.

Social Media and Portals

Most user-friendly portals now incorporate social media. Tools such as social networking groups allow employees to form internal affinity groups (all gamers or joggers), communities of practice (HR recruiting), or communities of learning (such as those interested in learning a new language). Blogging by the CEO or a corporation-wide wiki can increase the reach and power of the portal, both internally and externally. (For more information on social media, see Chapter 3.) Another related technology tip is to incorporate graphics, video, infographics, and other similar items. The more the site engages users (or is "sticky"), the more likely it is that the target audience will use the portal. Video clips and graphics attract attention and can convey a point. Podcasting can be used to capture the visitor's attention.

The GWU Internal Portal in Figure 11.1 does not use the methods of graphics video and other engaging "hooks," but what it lacks in flash it makes up in function. This is typical of an internal versus external portal. That said, a

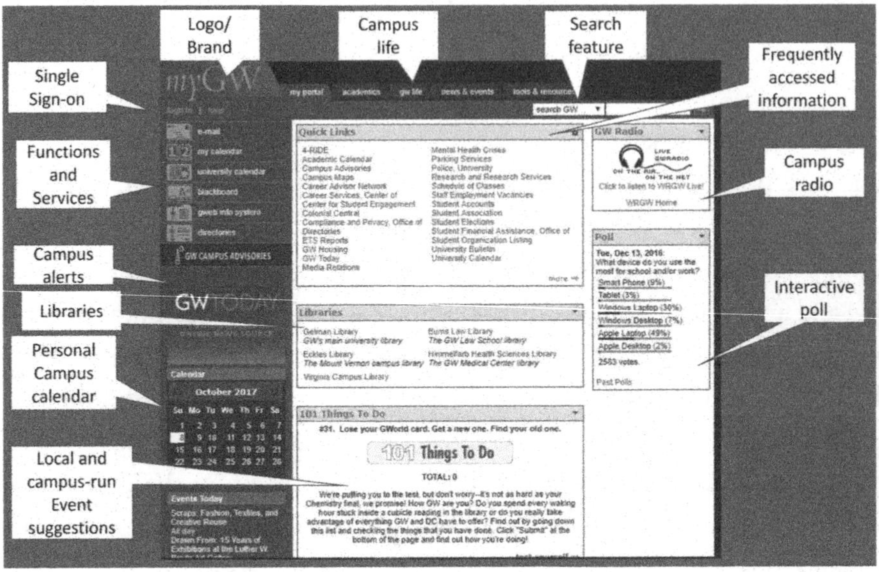

Figure 11.1: GWU Internal Portal

student can use this portal to access everything necessary for earning a degree without ever stepping foot on campus. That is a powerful portal!

THE HR PROFESSIONAL AND HR PORTALS

Portal design and redesign offer opportunities for collaboration. HR managers will find themselves working alongside those in the IT department; that is a given. However, other key players may include members of finance (for budget and cost), marketing, and graphics, as well as executives. The HR manager can provide insight into the most valuable in-house, HR-based functions and how they can be offered through the portal. Further, HR can offer informal learning opportunities (such as videos or blogs) with current information about the portal and how to maximize its potential.

A well-designed HR portal should eliminate much of the administrivia, the small routine but essential details, handled daily by HR personnel. Information about benefits, healthcare, and courseware for personal development can be offered to the internal audience by way of the portal. Knowing the core businesses within the organization enables the HR professional to target specific bodies of information that are valuable to the employee and that could impact job performance. For instance, if legislation exists that relates to the organization's goals and mission, the HR department could assist the developers in making that information available, along with other legal resources. Further, regular courseware or certification courseware can be advertised on the internal portal. Important communiqués relevant to the employees can be distributed through the portal. Thus, through input at the strategic level regarding the HR portal design, the HR professional can have a significant, positive impact.

The benefits of an HR portal cannot be denied. Since the cost of developing and maintaining a portal varies significantly by model used, some organizations choose to develop the portal in-house. Others turn to hosted services. In the latter case, the vendor handles the hardware and software for the newer dynamic features and functions. Subscription fees vary significantly, but if you do not have the in-house capabilities to develop a portal, then a vendor can fill those gaps.

EMPLOYEE SELF-SERVICE (ESS) PORTALS

For HR, the ESS portal is a real advantage. Self-serve portals offer a number of different functions and bring a wide variety of organizational resources, tools, and services directly to the employee's desktop. The same portal design principles pertain to the internal ESS portal. The feature that differentiates the ESS from a standard internal portal is that individual employees have access to their own HR information:

- Personal information
  - o Training and development status as well as offerings
  - o Benefits enrollment and benefits services
  - o Tax-related changes (e.g., change to dependent or marital status)
  - o Retirement information and access to 401(k) savings investment records
  - o Cost information on health plan alternatives (e.g., HMO, PPO)
- Personal data
  - o Emergency contact, address, telephone information
  - o Previous and current pay, performance, and time-tracking information
  - o Time reports, vacation or sick days, and travel expense reports

- Online learning (both internal and external courses)
- Onboarding and orientation activities
- Internal job vacancies
- Employment tests and certifications
- Organization-wide communications
- Company policies or procedures
- HR policy manuals and email inquiry or help request
- Employee surveys

Eugene Valeriano and Marlon Gamido provide the following advice regarding what *not* to do with your ESS portals: Do not make it into a link farm, providing links to enrollment forms, vendor pages, outdated information, basic benefits, and change-of-address forms. Instead provide access to services and applications that are useful to the intended audience.[122]

In an article about attracting talent, Karen Thoreson and Nijah Fudge describe the positive changes that resulted for an HR department in local government in Dallas, Texas, when they implemented an ESS portal.[123] Through the ESS, Dallas local government HR provides access to payroll, benefits, and HR policies and procedures and has the ability to update and print important documents. The Dallas city government cited an increase in productivity. Employees who were calling HR about information regarding payroll, benefits, and standard HR policies and procedures could go directly to their own records to access answers to questions. This freed up members of the HR department to their jobs, thereby increasing their productivity by eliminating time spent digging up answers to questions that the employees could access.

To measure the portal's usefulness, look at measures such as the employees' reactions to ease of use, reliability, accuracy, functionality, and security of the portal. These reactions can be gathered through a survey, poll, or other feedback mechanism embedded in the portal. IT experts involved in this effort will look for user interface, functionality, database design, and security.

MOBILE PORTALS

A mobile portal differs from any other type of portal in that it must be adapted to the mobile device, making it mobile accessible. The size of the screen on the mobile device impacts the design of a mobile portal. Specifically, the content must be stripped to a bare minimum. Too much information on the page can confuse the user, cause unnecessary delays in downloading, and even lock up the device. A well-designed mobile portal may look something like the one shown in Figure 11.2.

Portals can be used in a number of ways, as has been demonstrated throughout this chapter. The HR manager, armed with basic portal design information and a knowledge of HR, can provide insight into the most valuable in-house, HR-based functions and how they can be offered through the portal. Internal portals serve the employees by giving them more control

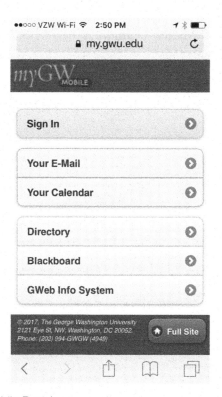

Figure 11.2. GWU Mobile Portal

over accessing personal information. ESS portals serve as a doorway to access all things HR, which empowers and engages the employee. Furthermore, the portal can be adapted for mobile entry enabled through the cloud.

End-of-Chapter Technology Strategy Questions

Considering your organization's overall business strategy and that of your HR department, as well as the needs of your employees, answer the following:

1. How could your organization benefit from the use of HR portals?
2. How could your organization use an ESS portal in its overall HR Technology Strategy?

Digging Deeper

Sullivan, Dan. 2009. *Proven Portals: Best Practices for Planning, Designing, and Developing Enterprise Portals*. Boston: Pearson Education.

Valeriano, Eugene, and Marlon Gamido. 2016. *HRIS, IPMIS and PS: An Integrated System with Employee Portal*. Saarbrücken, Deu.: Lambert Academic Publishing.

PART IV

KNOWLEDGE MANAGEMENT

CHAPTER 12

Managing Knowledge

TOPICS COVERED IN THIS CHAPTER

- Technical trends and knowledge management

- Knowledge hierarchy

- KM strategy components

- Knowledge networks

- HR's role in KM

- Soaring to new heights with KM: an airline's KM and an IT organization's KM—two cases

- KM's legal, ethical, and security challenges

- Measuring KM effectiveness

Knowledge management (KM) is neither a product nor a service, but rather a practice woven into the fabric of an organization. The concept of KM has been around since the twentieth century, although the practice of KM has changed considerably. Philip Harris, in his book *Managing the Knowledge Culture,* defines *knowledge management* as "the facilitation and support of the processes for creating, sustaining, sharing, and renewing organizational knowledge in order to generate economic wealth, create value, or improve performance."[124]

Knowledge management has become particularly important in order for organizations to remain viable and vibrant. Some experts say that the success and sustainability of an organization is largely due to whether or not it can create, capture, store, share, transfer, and use knowledge. HR is integral to establishing and perpetuating KM and especially knowledge sharing. For example, training during onboarding sets the tone for sharing knowledge. Additionally, positive reinforcement—in the form of rewards and emphasis on the mutual benefits to each individual and ultimately the entire organization—reinforces knowledge sharing. Job design, mobility, and programs such as apprenticeships can stimulate the transfer of knowledge. Similarly, communities of practice (CoPs) can be an environment for knowledge sharing. A *community of practice,* according to Wenger, McDermott, and Snyder, is a group of "people who share a concern, a set of problems, or a passion about a topic, and who deepen their knowledge and expertise in this area by interacting on an ongoing basis."[125]

In this chapter we will examine the knowledge hierarchy, KM components, supporting technology and two examples of successful KM deployments using very different technology strategies.

These are the obvious ways that HR can promote KM. However, simply using these methods will not ensure their success. Truly embedded and integral KM must be intentional. Additionally, employees must understand the benefits of KM, both to them personally and to the organization. KM technology platforms should be integrated with the daily workflow. There should be resources designated to sustaining KM. Implementation should not be relegated to the IT department; rather, HR must be lead.

Knowledge management will only succeed if there is thoughtful attention to the technology underpinnings. There are several critical requirements for a KM technology strategy. It should include

- A technology infrastructure that is integrated with current systems;
- Software that supports knowledge sharing both individually and in group settings;
- Consideration of a repository for knowledge;
- Security to protect private data and intellectual property;
- An educated employee base that understands the principles of knowledge management, how to contribute, and the benefits of doing so;
- Governance best practices;
- A gatekeeper or gatekeepers who support and enforce a structured KM approach that vets and maintains knowledge assets;
- Leadership support;
- A team of individual champions with the skills to promote and drive KM throughout the organization; and
- An agreed-upon method to measure the impact of KM.

TECHNOLOGY TRENDS AND KM

The KM system often uses a mixture of many of the technologies described in this text. Stephanie Barnes and Nick Milton, in their book *Designing a Successful KM Strategy*, provide a framework for the types of technologies and their use when implementing a knowledge management strategy. Those authors divide the technologies into four functions that allow users to (1) connect people to share knowledge, (2) allow collection of knowledge, (3) push knowledge, and (4) pull knowledge.[126] These four functions can be empowered by technology: knowledge "connection" and "sharing" can occur through the use of groupware and online discussion forums; knowledge can be "collected" through developing training, m-learning, and performance support tools; knowledge can be "pushed" out using blogs, chat, RSS feeds, and podcasts/vodcasts; and knowledge can be "pulled" through search features that allow the user to find specific resources.

Additionally, the technology trends discussed in this text empower the knowledge management process. KM systems can range in sophistication from a simple, organized Dropbox used as a repository that contains end-of-project debriefs, white papers, expert resources, presentations, and so on, or the use of a product like SharePoint which is readily available in the Microsoft suite of products and provides an integrated network for sharing knowledge. Or a knowledge portal for an HR system that offers a variety of data for analysis and creation of new knowledge (see Chapter 8). Behind the scenes, the Internet of Things can enable data gathering and machine learning, which can result in new knowledge.[127] Social networking, social media, groupware, blogs, wikis, and other technologies can be integrated into a knowledge management approach. Of course, making the KM system cloud-enabled and mobile accessible will increase its impact. There is no single right configuration for a knowledge management approach; the important thing is to have a KM strategy and implement it.

Your organization's mission and vision as well as its HR technology strategy should impact the design of the knowledge management system. Keeping the user in mind, the extent to which you can incorporate the technology trends of mobile, social, data analytics, IoT, and cloud computing and communicate the process of using and contributing to the KM system will make it more attractive and accessible to users.

KNOWLEDGE HIERARCHY

When building a knowledge strategy, it is important to remember that not all knowledge is of equal value. The knowledge hierarchy could be seen as a pyramid from bottom to top are data, information, knowledge, expertise and capability. At the bottom of that pyramid are data which can include images, facts, numeric codes, and texts, but data are relatively useless unless interpreted. One example of KM data are unexamined survey results. Information is data that has meaning to the user and has a context, an organization schema or directory for example. The next step in the hierarchy is knowledge itself that can be described as information that has been analyzed, understood, and interpreted. Interpretation is the key. Expertise occurs when the knowledge that has been understood is applied. This might be best practices that have been captured and codified, let's say regarding project management or onboarding or dealing with a particular client. Capability is when the knowledge has spread throughout the organization, resulting in a generalized practice.[128] Clearly the resulting capability is more valuable than raw data.

KM STRATEGY COMPONENTS

The new technology trends do not negate the best practices of knowledge management. Remember that a knowledge management system is not necessarily a technology in this case, although it can rely upon technology. Rather it is a strategy that, when implemented, impacts the way the organization views and handles its knowledge assets. Knowledge management systems enable the ability to create, capture, store, share, transfer, and use knowledge. Technology can assist with every step.

Some refer to this process as the cycle of knowledge; however, the process is not nearly that organized. The sequence does not drive the process. Every knowledge management strategy must include the ability to create, capture, store, share, and use:

- **Creation**. Knowledge creation can be achieved through research, problem-solving, action learning, innovation, and demonstration projects, to name a few methods.
- **Capture.** When assessing what knowledge we already have within an organization, we continually diagnose what should be collected or "captured"; in some cases the knowledge must be acquired.
- **Storage.** Storing the knowledge that the company creates or collects requires a plan. Typically, the explicit knowledge is stored in a database or data warehouse, but it can also be stored in something as simple as a Dropbox or server. Those not using technology may use a file cabinet. Knowledge management benefits from the use of technology to contain and retain knowledge.
- **Sharing and Transfer.** Sharing knowledge can be a controversial aspect of knowledge management. If knowledge is power, it makes sense that people would want to protect what knowledge they have or hoard it. One

way around knowledge hoarding is to incentivize and reward those who share and transfer knowledge.

- **Use/Application**. It is not enough for knowledge to be acquired, stored, shared, and transferred, it must be used in order to make the endeavor of KM worthwhile. Knowledge application depends on employees having efficient access to valuable knowledge. Two key practices that assist in knowledge use are data mining (which is dependent on a method of storing the data) and knowledge networks.[129]

KNOWLEDGE NETWORKS

Through integrated networks, knowledge can be made available anytime, anywhere, and in any form. Of course, the Internet and virtual private networks (VPNs) are critical to internal knowledge sharing. However, a knowledge network makes knowledge available. *Knowledge networks* are the backbone of the KM system because knowledge is accessed and used via a network that allows employees to share knowledge. Typically, the choice of network has already been made by the time the knowledge management system is conceived. Many organizations today use a cloud-enabled network to access the knowledge they have anywhere and anytime. Some knowledge networks rely upon tools such as Microsoft SharePoint. Knowledge networks do not need to be fancy or sophisticated; the goal of using networks for knowledge management is to, as they say, just do it.

A knowledge network can also be intangible, as in communities of practice (CoPs). CoPs provide a valuable way to share knowledge and can be assembled or facilitated by technology. Online CoPs are highly effective when developed and supported within an organization. Examples include project management CoPs, research CoPs, and best practices CoPs.

For a KM system to be successful, at the very least there must be a gatekeeper who oversees the network and ensures that the knowledge that is captured, stored, and shared is worthwhile and aligned with the organization's mission, vision, and goals. Without a gatekeeper (or multiple gatekeepers), the knowledge repository can become a disorderly dumping ground. Clearly defined submission procedures for submitting knowledge assets to the KM system serve to protect the quality of the knowledge. A periodic purge of outdated and unused information is the gatekeeper's responsibility. Be sure you establish who will be the gatekeeper(s) and the rules for submission to the KM system. This could be the role of someone in HR. HR must be a strategic partner in the KM process as well as an advocate. Having visibility and oversight in a role such as gatekeeper or in the governance process ensures HR's involvement as decision makers.

TIPS AND TOOLS FOR KM

- KM requires forethought, planning, a strategy, and leadership support.
- The knowledge management system must relate to and support organizational goals.
- Existing systems and expertise within an organization should be used as sources of knowledge.
- The KM system needs to be structured, monitored, and maintained to be useful.
- Gatekeepers and a governance team provide oversight and ongoing strategies to manage and increase the usefulness of the KM system.
- The KM system should allow for knowledge creating, capturing/collecting, storing, sharing and transferring, and applying.
- HR must be a strategic partner in the KM process as well as an advocate.

HR'S ROLE IN KM

The KM system can ultimately be used by every group within the organization. The more useful the information, the more people will want access to the KM system. Any group or division within the organization that will access KM should have a representative and advocate involved in its design. Of course, there will be ongoing interactions with the IT professionals, but there may also be work with the financial and marketing departments as well as graphics and any other group in the organization who will benefit from using the KM system. HR should be involved in all aspects of the KM system. It is sometimes easy to relinquish control to the business units; however, the role of business partner dictates that HR participate. Oversight of the KM ensures involvement.

Computer Systems That Support KM

Surprisingly, legacy systems can contribute to the KM process because they store the lessons learned from past business endeavors. Other systems commonly leveraged for knowledge management include LCMSs, HR systems (HRISs, talent management systems [TMSs], HCM systems) and client relationship management (CRM) systems. The LCMS collects knowledge through the courses offered and provides an indicator of the knowledge deemed important enough to disseminate. The TMS, HCM system, or HRIS provides abundant performance information that can be used to identify experts, top performers, and teams that are considered sources of knowledge. The HR system specifically can cultivate knowledge by making accessible directories or databases with contact information linked to knowledge providers via a knowledge map. The CRM systems offer a wealth of knowledge in the shape of feedback from clients through blogs, surveys, chat, and so on. That feedback, when analyzed, becomes new knowledge.

Customer or Client Relationship Management (CRM)

A *CRM system* "lets you store and manage prospect and customer information, like contact info, accounts, leads, and sales opportunities, in one central location."[130] The CRM system technology is software that tracks customer interactions. It is useful for customer service, sales, marketing, and KM. For knowledge management purposes, a CRM system can supply valuable information that provides insight into the habits, preferences, and needs of the client. The customer information that is gleaned through this system can inform sales activities. The CRM also contains sales tools to track customer profiles, feedback, customer calls, proposals, and other important data. The knowledge contained in the CRM can be accessed at any time. Many CRMs are now cloud-enabled and mobile accessible and so is the dashboard, summary level information that an organization can glean for the data in the CRM. While this is outside the typical domain of HR, the fact that the CRM can be used as a KM tool by HR's business partners increases the need to be aware of HR's contribution to its oversight.

CASE STUDY

Soaring to New Heights with KM: An Airline's KM and a Technology Organization's KM—Two Cases

Organizations and entire economies benefit both economically and socially from knowledge management. At least, this was the position of one Middle Eastern country that began a nationwide knowledge management initiative, rewarding organizations that pursued and implemented a KM strategy. An international airline in that Middle Eastern country was handling and storing knowledge using paper-based storage cabinets. Spurred by the government initiative to improve digital advancement, the airlines implemented a strategic KM approach that incorporated current technologies.

The knowledge management approach relies predominantly upon Yammer and SharePoint. Yammer (Microsoft's intraorganizational social networking program) is used to send employees updates on specific topics of business interest. Employees discuss and contribute to topics or comment from their experience or expertise in Yammer. Discussion topics include everything from internal projects, news, crisis management, personal knowledge and development, and aviation current events.

Organization-wide use of SharePoint also allows employees to view and share resources. Predetermined access levels are embedded in the system. Employees conduct synchronous chat as well as share files and documents pertaining to current business initiatives within the airline.

This KM system, reliant on social media and social networking, has delivered positive results. Employees provided ideas for improvements, many of which have subsequently been acted upon. Across departments, communication has increased significantly and organizational silos have been eradicated. Concerns aired via internal social media have also been addressed. Corporate messages on policy changes, newsletters and procedures are now reliant upon the organization's knowledge management strategy to provide a uniform message and branding for the airline.

A major finding from this knowledge management endeavor was that KM generates a spirit of collaboration and internal organizational socializing. The employee engagement ratings reportedly soared. This follows the research that states that knowledge sharing bears a direct, positive relationship to employee job satisfaction and engagement.

Representing a different approach to knowledge management is an IT organization that wanted to provide better, more current resources for their sales and marketing team. The need was for the team to have current information about customers, potential customers, and entire industries as well as past proposals offered to specific customers and any current developments with those customers.

As a solution, the IT department developed a knowledge portal that provides sales professionals valuable knowledge assets to better serve current and potential clients. Included in the portal are a variety of features:

- Dashboards from the LMS and CRM system in one summary format with drill-down capability for sales by customer;
- A personalized training map of completed and suggested courses;
- Social networking features that allow employees to chat with executives and experts;
- RSS news feeds, telephone, and updates based on categories of information relevant to the sales professional;
- Knowledge resources such as the organization's policies, procedures, solutions, and communications;
- Click-to-chat, which captures employee questions into a searchable database of frequently asked questions and answers;
- An advanced search engine to access specific knowledge management resources;
- Personalization that adapts to the unique interests of the individual; and
- An Employee Service Center that offers access to individual timekeeping, scheduling, benefits, and learning opportunities.

The comparison of these two knowledge management systems demonstrates viable and effective designs ranging from relatively simple (airline) to more complex (IT organization). The point is that both organizations achieved their KM objectives. A KM system should provide the information and tools that the employees need to make informed decisions.

KM'S LEGAL, ETHICAL, AND SECURITY CHALLENGES

Legal and ethical limits to sharing knowledge exist. Let's start with the legal arena. In the arena of medicine and health sciences in the United States, HIPAA is an ongoing concern for those involved in records management. This act is a federal law, part of which mandated that the Department of Health and Human Services had to establish rules that would improve the dissemination of healthcare information while protecting the privacy of individuals.

Those who work in the fields of health sciences and medicine in the United States are very aware of this act and its importance. However, other industries are not immune to the potential legal ramifications of displaying private information on a knowledge network. In fact, HR departments in for profit, nonprofit, public, and private organizations all handle personal and private information that should not be shared, transferred, or collected on a knowledge management system. Proper thresholds of access should be in place if information has to be shared over a network. Any KM system dealing with private, personal information must be secure and protected from piracy, invasion via malware, or any other threats to corruption or abrogated security of important and private data.

This leads directly to the issue of the ethics involved in knowledge sharing. With regard to ethics and knowledge sharing, we mentioned earlier the issues surrounding social media. The organization must have clear policies indicating what can and cannot be shared over the knowledge network. There should be protocols for submission that involve a vetting process that would catch any potential ethical issues. System access to the knowledge network should involve levels of access based on job title and responsibility. It is impossible to control the behavior of participants in a knowledge network, but having policies, protocols, and system access thresholds based on job title and, in the case of government, clearance levels can curb unethical behavior and allow for follow-up actions if unethical activities occur.

KM System Vulnerabilities

The issue of protecting private data is not limited to one industry or organization; it has relevance across the board. Three key areas of vulnerability for any computer or knowledge management system include the threat of piracy, potential invasions of privacy, and breaches of security involving online information. Each of these threats is explained below.

Piracy

Piracy is the illegal copying of software or unauthorized use of material from computer or online sources. Some ways to prevent piracy include obtaining licenses, locking hard disks, limiting access to information, and educating employees on the organization's software use policies. US copyright laws make it illegal to put large portions of copyrighted text or images on the Internet (or to otherwise republish it). The fair use doctrine and the TEACH Act (described in detail in Chapter 5) offer some limited exceptions to copyright. Most universities deal with copyright infringement laws by educating their students on the law, its ramifications, and how to avoid copyright infringement. Additionally, university library representatives model the correct approach by posting copyrighted materials in a way that abides by copyright laws. HR departments would do well to follow the same guidelines in oversight of a KM system.

Invasion of Privacy

Data privacy pertains to the employee, member, or student information often kept in databases. In many databases, it is easy to track what the users are doing, but individuals must be warned that online actions are being recorded and may be examined. Any information captured without an established policy and employees' foreknowledge of that policy is considered an invasion of privacy. For organizations, this is an important aspect of software and Internet usage. The protection of privacy begins with an organization having a clearly stated policy regarding what can and cannot be shared.

Security Breaches

Security breaches are more likely if there are no access levels built into the system. This can be handled by a knowledge portal where the login identifies the user and their level of access. However, there are also situations where unethical workers practicing information mining can gather private data without permission or proper notifications. This is an ongoing challenge that can be mitigated in the hiring process with background checks, but there is no foolproof guard against such activity. Security breaches via unauthorized people accessing information can be prevented by using firewalls. These are technological barriers designed to prevent unwanted communications between computer networks or hosts. They are established by the IT department. They prevent outside attempts at breaches, but cannot be used to guard against internal issues. Multiple sign-on levels can prevent access from unwanted actors to systems and data but that makes the access more difficult.

Threats to KM Systems

Threats to KM systems include computer viruses and worms. A *computer virus* is a software program that is designed to spread like a highly contagious illness from one computer to another and interfere with computer functions. A virus may corrupt or delete data on a computer, use an email program to spread itself to other computers, or even erase everything on the hard disk. Computer viruses spread through infected attachments in email messages or instant messaging messages. That is why it is essential that you never open an email attachment unless you know the sender and you are expecting it. Viruses can be disguised as attachments of funny images, greeting cards, or audio or video files.

A *computer worm* is a malware program that self-replicates. It uses a network to send copies of itself to other computers on the network; it may do so without any user intervention. The worm is successful when there are insufficient malware or antivirus protections or those in place are not up-to-date. Unlike a virus, a computer worm does not need to attach itself to an existing program. Worms almost always cause at least some harm to the network, even if only by occupying bandwidth. Since they are usually attached to software, the gatekeeper must set and enforce standard procedures for submitting KM assets so that there are proper protocols for submission and it is clear what can be submitted.

MEASURING KM EFFECTIVENESS

It is always wise to evaluate the effectiveness of an HR initiative, in this case knowledge management. Relevant metrics that will help you evaluate the usage and overall performance include a variety of well-used and reliable measures as well as one that is unique to KM:[131]

- Facets of the KM that align with organizational goals.
- Surveys and social media to evaluate the quality and the accessibility of the KM content.
- Response rate for request for improvement or need for more information.
- IT records demonstrating system problems.

End-of-Chapter Technology Strategy Questions

Considering your organization's overall business strategy and the technology strategy of your HR department, answer the following:

1. How does your organization handle KM, and what role does HR play in KM?
2. How could HR increase the exchange of knowledge within the organization?
3. What new KM processes, policies, and technologies would increase the effectiveness of the organization's KM?

Digging Deeper

Barnes, Stephanie, and Nick Milton. 2016. *Designing a Successful KM Strategy: A Guide for the Knowledge Management Professional.* Medford, NJ: Information Today.

Haimila, Sandra. 2017. "Trend-Setting Products of 2017." *KM World,* September 14, 2017. http://www.kmworld.com/Articles/Editorial/Features/KMWorld-Trend-Setting-Products-of-2017-120392.aspx.

Harris, Philip Robert. 2005. *Managing the Knowledge Culture: A Guide for Human Resource Professionals and Managers in the 21st Century Workplace.* Amherst: HRD Press Inc.

CHAPTER 13

Groupware for Collaboration

TOPICS COVERED IN THIS CHAPTER

- What is groupware?

- Mobile and cloud-enabled groupware

- Virtual teams and CoPs

- Virtual conferences and meetings

- Knowledge management, social learning, and groupware

- An innovative case using groupware for knowledge management and employee learning and development

Virtual teams and the growth of communities of practice (CoPs) have spurred technological innovations in communication and collaboration. Groupware is one such innovation. The term *groupware* "refers to programs that help people work together collectively while located remotely from each other."[132] Groupware enables ongoing virtual communication and collaboration. It has become indispensable as a business tool for a broad spectrum of uses including instruction, virtual project teams, meetings, webinars, and even action learning. (The latter methodology is based on asking questions in a group setting to elicit new, innovative solutions.[133]) It is also valuable as a KM tool to create and capture new knowledge generated by affinity groups and CoPs within an organization.

This chapter defines groupware and explains its importance for the virtual workplace and knowledge management in general and virtual teams and CoPs in particular. The case study of a government agency demonstrates innovative use of groupware for employee learning and development purposes.

WHAT IS GROUPWARE?

Groupware is collaborative software (also referred to as workgroup support systems or simply group support systems) designed to help people involved in a common task achieve their goals. Groupware often incorporates video, chat, instant messaging, polling capabilities, emoticons for feedback, hotlinks for virtual tours, and whiteboards, as well as presentation software. It may rely on both telecommunication and the Internet or strictly on the Internet. The goal in using groupware is to enable interaction between individuals or groups that are not colocated.

Advantages and Disadvantages of Groupware

Groupware offers a variety of benefits. The software allows users to give slide presentations, use drawing tools, conduct demos, and collaborate in real time on projects when the participants are not in the same location. The groupware can support a wide variety of applications—everything from training in a social learning context, to collaborating with virtual teams, to promoting and coordinating CoPs. There are also cost benefits to groupware:

groupware allows organizations to cut down on the cost of travel both in real dollars and lost productivity time.[134]

The drawbacks of groupware are less obvious. As with any other technology, it is important to select the groupware that is best suited to and most compatible with the technology infrastructure, organizational context, and culture. Additionally, groupware-enabled interactions should be designed with the features of the tool in mind. Training may be needed in order to bring all stakeholders up to the same level of functionality. It is essential that use of the groupware be planned and intentional. Failing to choose groupware that can be used by all, disregarding the need for initial training on the groupware, and a lack of preparation for and adjustment of the presentation approach to maximize the features of the groupware can cause even the best groupware to be underutilized.

When using groupware, here are some helpful guidelines. If the groupware does not have a video component, introduce yourself before speaking. As the presenter, avoid long presentations (over 30–45 minutes). Audiences quickly lose interest when there is no interaction. Regularly gauge participant involvement by asking questions and polling for response. Document the audience chat response and questions, then ensure that you respond to each question. With smaller audiences you may release the microphone and let audience members comment or contribute using their own microphones. However, for larger audiences (or if the message requires a one-way communication), disable microphones for everyone except the presenter. Engage the audience by using polling features, roll call, and questions to increase the social presence and sense of immediacy.

MOBILE AND CLOUD-ENABLED GROUPWARE

Most mobile groupware is cloud enabled, which allows participants to access groupware on their mobile devices. Collaborate Ultra, FaceTime, and GoToMeeting are groupware that enable mobile access to both the presenter and the presentations. The physical constraints of mobile devices (limited display size, power, and memory capacity) must be taken into consideration when sharing information in presentation format because some mobile devices cannot receive the same amount or format of information as a desktop. Additionally, since mobile device users may move and change location, they may experience interrupted service. That being said, an entire suite of groupware is available and tailored to the mobile user, an important consideration if your potential audience is frequently on the road or off-site and you intend to provide them with groupware access.

TIPS AND TOOLS FOR USING GROUPWARE

When you examine groupware for adoption by your organization, consider your answers to the following questions:

- How will your company use the groupware?

- Where will the software be rolled out in its pilot form, and what will the process be after that?

- Are all of the computers and mobile devices used by employees compatible with the groupware?

- Who will use this tool for remote collaboration?

- Will all users be in-house or will collaboration include clients?

- How will the groupware provider or your organization address security needs?

- How many participants will you have and how often? Does the number of participants impact license and cost?

- How complicated is the installation, and will the users need assistance or training to use groupware?

VIRTUAL TEAMS AND CoPS

A *virtual team* is defined as "a group of skilled individuals who communicate electronically."[135] According to this and many current definitions, "virtualness" is the defining characteristic and a potential characteristic of any modern team. For the purposes of this text, we will refer to teams interacting virtually (i.e., in the online or computer-based realm) as virtual teams. Hybrid teams, while challenging, are defined as teams that are managed with both colocated team members and global team members. Global organizations often have hybrid virtual teams.

There are numerous challenges to operating virtual teams. Virtual teams do not have the benefit of in-person interactions. Cultural differences on global teams can cause conflicts, and there is an absence of body language cues that could offset the potential conflicts. There is the potential for social isolation. Trust issues can arise because there is no way to see what teammates are doing, and time differences can impact work hours so that you are not working at the same time. These conditions, if not addressed, can breed discord.

However, well-run virtual teams can be very satisfying, and they certainly offer cost benefits for the organization as well as round-the-clock workforce availability and the opportunity to find expertise anywhere in the world. Some benefits for the individual include the time and schedule flexibility and a higher level of responsibility, which result in work motivation and the empowerment of team members.[136]

Virtual team leadership requires a unique set of skills that differ from those required for leadership in a face-to-face environment. What follows are guidelines distilled from a variety of sources that contain common themes. Virtual team leaders should set ground rules, including clearly delineated tasks, deliverables, commitments, agreed-upon and consistent communication practices, role division, time management techniques, and feedback. There should be specificity and commitment to the agreed-upon ground rules that take the form of a team charter. The team lead should think more structure, not less. If possible, try to have at least two members working together at every location. Overcommunicate to try to limit the side conversations. Maintain the original team boundaries by not adding team members.

VIRTUAL CONFERENCES AND MEETINGS

Technology is obviously of great importance for virtual teams. The technologies that are useful for virtual teams can also be extended to handle virtual conferences and large, virtual meetings. Groupware, such as Skype for Business, GoToMeeting, and WebEx, provide particularly powerful technology options. Web conferencing is a type of groupware where a presenter can deliver a presentation over the web to a group of geographically dispersed participants. In its simplest form, the presentation is not interactive: participants can see what's on the screen but cannot make changes. In its most sophisticated form, there are embedded features that allow for polling, chat, screen display, collaboration on a document, video display, and telephone or voice over Internet protocol (VoIP).

The desktop use of webcam and computer with Internet connection has made videoconferencing more cost effective. Videoconferencing allows users to see and hear each other as they interact. A simple example of this form of videoconferencing over the Internet is offered by Microsoft Skype for business or the open-source software FaceTime, and there are others emerging as well. Enabled by the cloud, web conferencing extends to all areas of the globe. It is often used in webinars where what would normally be a seminar is delivered using a web-conferencing tool. Note that there may be a limit to the audience size based on licensing agreements and/or the parameters directed by the system. In any case, it is a cost-effective tool for meetings, especially in lieu of travel costs for participants.

Some organizations are even conducting large conferences online rather than face-to-face. Tools like Avaya Scopia offers telecommunications connectivity for groups, meetings, and even conferences. Imagine the travel savings possible by handling large conferences virtually rather than face-to-face. Break-out rooms and smaller sessions can also be conducted concurrently using these advanced videoconferencing tools.

Meetings can be handled using virtual online groupware when talking to employees in person isn't an option. "It's what we can call 'virtual face time,' " says Kimberly Elsbach, an organizational behavior expert at the University of California-Davis. "It has some of the same benefits as being in person."[137]

The virtual online groupware also may include other features in addition to the presentation software. Virtual polling embedded in the groupware can be used for polling the audience and decision-making. Other compatible tools include Google Docs for modifying documents. Online calendaring or scheduling can be used to communicate meeting changes or to schedule the next meeting. The videoconference feature included in some groupware enables relationship building through face-to-face interaction and can also allow for discussion. The chat feature in some web conferencing tools allows the audience to pose questions during the presentation for the presenter to address or the team members to discuss after the presentation.

KNOWLEDGE MANAGEMENT, SOCIAL LEARNING, AND GROUPWARE

Social learning can be facilitated through web-enabled videoconferencing groupware, as the learners experience immediate feedback through that media. Participant learners share insights that benefit the group as well as its attendees. These sessions can be captured and saved. The saved version can become a knowledge asset and shared in whatever format (whether a file or URL) over the knowledge network. The experience of "social presence" can be accomplished through teleconferencing or videoconferencing, but the media that are richer in facial and verbal expression are optimal for learning in a social (rather than individual) context.[138]

CASE STUDY

An Innovative Case Using Groupware for Knowledge Management and Employee Learning and Development

Skyler Heavans

The US Government Accountability Office (GAO) has a workforce of about three thousand federal and contract employees with its headquarters located in Washington, DC, and eleven field offices spread across the country. Often referred to as the "congressional watchdog," GAO advises Congress on recommendations for solving problems in government programs and operations that involve taxpayer dollars. A legislative agency with a workforce of acute critical thinkers, GAO is a true learning organization that requires its employees to complete continuing professional education credits on a two-year cycle. This constant learning drives performance improvement and innovation. With over 250 agency-specific courses ranging from analyst or auditor training to technical and soft-skill classes and a comprehensive leadership program, the agency constantly seeks effective ways to deliver its courses in a rapidly growing digital world. The primary driver of the agency's virtual paradigm shift was its telework program that launched in 2010 and the technology necessary to support it. As the agency's employees gradually increased their participation in telework, GAO adopted new technologies to meet the needs of the remote workforce. This included the deployment of an agency-wide virtual desktop interface (VDI)—a cloud-based computing environment—and other applications that nurtured an effective virtual learning environment (VLE). Such applications included a synchronous web collaboration platform that would support active learning to a growing number of online students both at its headquarters and field offices.

Even with a geographically dispersed workforce, GAO's organizational structure has never functioned in silos, especially when it comes to technology support and communication. The agency has a robust learning center that serves its VLE by providing quality learning through a variety of blended modalities such as classroom training, webinars, and e-learning. Continuous collaboration with its IT department has been the learning center's hallmark, as it is necessary to bridge the gaps between VDI and VLE, enabling the unit to provide job-transfer solutions to its expanding telework employees. When it came to selecting a virtual groupware platform, the learning center considered a number of requirements, such as multimedia and audio customization, breakout rooms, reporting, and necessary security protocols. As a leader in diversity and inclusion that fuels talent development, the agency implemented a number of internal feedback data collection systems so that employees at all levels of the organization had a voice in the agency's learning culture and its effect on their products, which predominantly include reports and testimonies to Congress. As such, all key personnel have been involved in creating a flexible work-life environment that swiftly responds to congressional needs. This is one of the many reasons why GAO is consistently ranked one of the best places to work in the federal government.

In 2017, GAO advanced its policies on telework arrangements and position suitability and launched an expanded telework program at its headquarters. Prior to the expansion of the telework program, the agency was prepared to confront any challenge to providing faster, easier, and more cost-efficient ways to train and collaborate with their virtual workforce. The progression of its telework program was predominantly made possible by GAO's cloud computing VDI structure, which enabled convenient, on-demand network access to a shared pool of computing resources with minimal management effort. VDI enhanced the swift deployment of many compatible learning applications, including online meeting platforms such as WebEx. However, to support live virtual classes across devices and the GAO network, the agency acquired Adobe

Connect as an SaaS COTS product to deliver a multitude of webinars that included topics on enhancing work in a virtual environment, such as "Connecting Teams at a Distance" and "Giving Feedback and Coaching in a Virtual Environment." Through a flipped pedagogical classroom model, these webinars have been successfully providing their agency's managers with the knowledge, confidence, and competence to best lead in a virtual context.

Acquiring a cloud-training service such as Adobe Connect has been one of GAO's best-value examples of supporting its VLE by providing engaging, live virtual learning to its remote workforce, all the while reducing travel costs for participants and instructors, and supporting equitable training for its eleven field offices. All in all, when it comes to collaboration and information sharing, the needs of HR and talent development will certainly evolve, shifting the balance of brick-and-mortar locations to virtual workspaces, capital investments to operational expenditures. More and more organizations will opt to rent rather than own their servers and software. GAO has been no different, continuously seeking ways to lessen their need to design, build, and maintain systems with demanding uptime and reliability requirements on their premises. Like many other similar institutions, GAO thrived during the digital industry's rapid evolution in the 1990s (which resulted in the Internet) and the following "Web 2.0," which led to social networking solutions, such as Facebook and Twitter. While we accept that the digital era has only just begun, technology (e.g., AI) will always be unpredictable—and in some instances, volatile—in its ability to meet the needs of learners and end users alike. But it's the human aspect (emotional intelligence) of organizational readiness and change management caused by technological advancement that will ultimately drive the success of the inevitable paradigm shifts ahead. GAO has been this constant model of organizational elasticity and learning that understands its reality, expanding its digital ecosystem accordingly.

Skyler Heavans, GAO Learning Center's Assistant Director for Instructional Design and Learning Technologies, is responsible for overseeing and directing the design, development, and delivery of GAO's talent development programs, compliance e-learning courses, and various other blended learning products and events.

• • • • • • • • • •

Groupware offers powerful conferencing, collaboration, knowledge management, learning, and synchronous communication capabilities. Groupware comes in a variety of forms, each of which has its benefits and shortcomings. When determining whether or not groupware is appropriate, always consider your audience, their level of comfort with the technology and their access to it, existing infrastructure, and the cost.

End-of-Chapter Technology Strategy Questions

Considering your organization's overall business strategy and HR's technology strategy, answer the following:

1. How does your organization presently train, collaborate, and share knowledge with remote employees who are not colocated?
2. How might groupware extend, support, and/or improve knowledge management, learning management and talent management within your organization?
3. How could groupware align with and enhance your HR technology strategy?

Digging Deeper

Lee, Margaret R. 2014. *Leading Virtual Project Teams: Adapting Leadership Theories and Communications Techniques to 21st Century Organizations.* Best Practices and Advances in Program Management Series. Boca Raton: CRC Press.

CHAPTER 14

Technology-Enabled Evaluation and Feedback

TOPICS COVERED IN THIS CHAPTER

- Evaluation and knowledge management in organizations

- Evaluation in organizations

- Evaluation methods and tools

- Evaluation, big data, and data analytics

- Dashboards and reports

- Performance management (PM)

- Case study of a global conglomerate redesigning its PM approach

- Mobile audience response polling systems

- Surveys and questionnaires

It is important to evaluate HR interventions of all kinds in order to examine their effectiveness and whether they have accomplished the stated goal. One facet of evaluation involves gathering feedback. This can be a tedious process when not assisted by technology. Thankfully, there are useful technologies for collecting feedback and evaluation data.

In this chapter we will examine the topic of evaluation methods and tools as applied from the micro to the macro level (individual performance feedback, to classroom polling, to organization-wide surveys) and how technology can be leveraged to support these efforts. A case study of a global conglomerate's radical transformation to continuous performance management shows how technology can support a complete culture change.

THE VALUE OF HUMAN CAPITAL

It has become increasingly evident that employees, or human capital, are the greatest asset of an organization. An entire body of literature has evolved on how to develop human capital and how quality and dedication of an organization's employees can impact an organization's performance. This shift, coupled with the development of high-powered technologies that support employee development, explains in part the recent propulsion of HR into the limelight. It also led to the rising importance of the HR department and HR executives as decision makers.

Nomenclature aside, organizations must recognize the employee as an important resource, over and above equipment, programs, and products. Organizational effectiveness rises and falls on the ability of the HR strategy to hire, onboard, assist, develop, and offboard employees, handling all aspects of the employee life cycle.

EVALUATION AND KNOWLEDGE MANAGEMENT IN ORGANIZATIONS

There are many different forms of evaluation. In this chapter, we examine evaluation at the individual, group and organization levels, but first we need to define the term. What is evaluation? Darlene Russ-Eft and Hallie Preskill define evaluation as a systematic process that is purposeful, involves collecting data regarding questions or issues, and requires judgment about the evaluee's merit, worth, or value. The end result should enhance knowledge and decision-making.[139]

Evaluation occurs within and outside organizations in many forms using different levels of analysis, including product evaluation, service evaluation, process evaluation, program evaluation, course evaluation, and evaluation of individual performance. Why do we evaluate? What are our reasons? We evaluate because doing so[140]

- Confirms results,
- Measures effectiveness,
- Assesses quality,
- Contributes to organization members' increased knowledge,
- Helps prioritize resources,
- Impacts planning for organizational change initiatives,
- Increases accountability, and
- May indicate a need for redirection.

EVALUATION METHODS

There are several evaluation and assessment methods. While the methods are all acceptable for HR purposes, the type of data being collected will impact the choice of method for data collection. Data types and methods for analysis appear below:[141]

- **Archival data.** Typically documents and records, nothing new is introduced in the data set. Evaluation is retrospective and based on the extant data. These sets may be combined and analyzed in new ways.
- **Modified archival data.** These are documents and records that may be added to and expanded. Analysis is done of the entire set of extant and new documents and records.
- **Observation in natural settings.** Evaluation data is gathered based on descriptions of behavior, not provided in current records.
- **Observation of artificial or simulated situations.** Special situations or stimuli are introduced and an observer (nonparticipant) records

notes on the respondent's behavior and reaction. Data are gathered by an evaluator.

- **Surveys and questionnaires.** These are special instruments that are developed for respondent completion. Evaluation is based on the survey's resultant data.
- **Testing.** Testing occurs to evaluate or assess knowledge or skills. Resulting data from the tests are examined.
- **Interviews, both individual and focus group.** After developing an interview guide, the interview is conducted. Data resulting from the interview are evaluated.
- **Polling.** In the context of HR, polls are snapshots of opinion at a point in time. Data resulting from the poll are typically aggregated by the tool.

While the methods have remained relatively constant, the technologies used for data collection and data analysis have changed.

EVALUATION, BIG DATA, AND DATA ANALYTICS

Evaluation data gathered using the methodologies described above can appear in two different formats: structured or unstructured.[142] Techopedia explains that *unstructured data* refers to data that follows a form that is either text or nontext. Text form include Word documents, PowerPoint presentations, instant messages, collaboration software, documents, books, social media posts. Nontext unstructured data are media such as MP3 audio files, JPEG images, and Flash video files.[143]

Structured data on the other hand are sometimes referred to as traditional data, "consisting mainly of text files that include well-organized information. Spreadsheets would be considered structured data; it can be arranged in a relational database system. Structured data is typically stored in a database or data warehouse from which it can be pulled for analysis. Legacy data mining and analytics solutions work with structured data."[144]

Data Sources and Storage

Evaluation efforts can result in structured or unstructured data depending upon the tools and methods used for data collection. New data sources are coming from streaming data from social media, mobile apps, locations services, and IoT. Methods for managing and analyzing the data depend upon the data format. Different data formats require different tools for analysis. Similar to the marketing branch of any organization, twenty-first-century HR departments rely on data to produce insights that lead to action. As the desire for more unstructured data grows, so does the need for new, effective ways of handling that data. Data warehouses are insufficient to handle the data types organizations want to analyze; thus, data lakes emerged.[145] *Data lake architecture* "is a store-everything approach to big data. Data are not classified when they are stored in the repository, as the value of the data is not clear at the outset. As a result, data preparation is eliminated."[146] A data lake can contain both structured and unstructured data.

Data Analysis Output—Dashboards and Reports

As the types of data resulting from data collection have changed, so has the final output resulting from the analysis. This is where the power of data is most readily seen. If the data are collected through the use of, for instance, a talent management system (TMS), you will have a broad range of reports and dashboards available based on the data residing in a single source. Where this comes into play is, for instance, in data collection for HR functions such as performance management. An HR department might want aggregated information about performance levels within a department, top performers, number of raises given, or manager coaching hours, and it may want that data reported by department. The TMS may provide that in report and/or dashboard format. All of that information is valuable for leadership to collect, compare, and act upon. As such, the output becomes a knowledge asset that could be a part of the knowledge management process.

Many standalone online or mobile survey tools used frequently for employee engagement surveys and the like also analyze the data and present it in bar charts, pie charts, and summary-level reports. For summary-level, unstructured data analytics, organizations like Glassdoor that compile feedback about organizations can also provide output in meaningful form with ratings and an examination of unstructured data, such as comments about organizations. Those resulting Glassdoor unstructured (comments) and structured (ratings) data become feedback for an organization that is again a knowledge asset that can be shared, stored, and acted upon.

There are three ways in which HR collects and maintains evaluation information: performance management (with a supporting case), audience response polls, and surveys. For each, we will describe the HR function and then discuss the tools and applications for HR. We will start with PM, an HR function dramatically impacted by the changing workplace and technology. Remember that feedback of all kinds can provide valuable knowledge that should be captured and used.

PERFORMANCE MANAGEMENT

Performance management is more important now than ever before. A ground shift occurred over the past several years. The performance management practices of conducting yearly reviews, implementing forced or stacked rankings, using a bell-curve to determine who gets bonuses or raises (or not), and examining past performance to make present judgments are falling by the wayside.[147] To replace these practices, organization like GE Microsoft, Netflix, Google,[148] Goldman, Adobe, IBM, Cisco,[149] and others have transformed their performance review process. Before discussing the value of the performance management tool as a data collection tool, let's first explain how the process is changing.

Susan Milligan of SHRM provides the guidance on how performance management sessions should be conducted: "Feedback must become more fluid."[150] It should be continuous. Employees should be encouraged to collaborate and contribute to the team and organization success rather than pitted against each other. The annual performance assessment is going away: studies indicate that at least 65 percent of employees want more feedback.[151]

Nina Mehta, in an article on performance management for the *Training Journal,* describes the new performance management approach as relational managers must take on more of a coaching role with their employees, "fostering a two-way exchange that builds communication and trust."[152] Managers are encouraged to[153]

- Emphasize strengths (rather than gaps),
- Match the timeline and milestones of projects with more frequent feedback rather than being rigid and date specific (such as giving performance once or twice a year),
- Make the performance management process engaging with open discussion and a structured record of goals and progress, and
- Put learning and development at the core while aligning performance goals with organizational outcomes that are measurable.

Clearly stated, until recently many organizations followed (and many still follow) a philosophy of performance management that demotivated, rather than motivated, employees. In the past five years, organizations have begun to realize the relationship between performance management practices and employee retention and engagement. The new perspective is that performance reviews can drive employee engagement, and engagement is connected to market performance because the more engaged the employee is, the more productive the employee is.

As mentioned above, the movement is toward "continuous performance management."[154] This means not only having more frequent conversations, but also holding more frequent goal-setting sessions with the employee. Ongoing coaching is recommended for employee development. Immediate (rather than delayed) feedback should be provided by the manager. Opportunities for continuous learning and development should be offered and based on regular discussions about capabilities and skills. Peer feedback can be part of the PM mix and offered through recognition tools. Recognition by management is based on performance, and feedback focuses on strengths and career aspirations, with "frequent check-ins and a developmental focus."[155] These policies are grounded in the literature on talent management.

Of course, a major change in performance management necessitates using a system that can accommodate the approach. This may impact the selection of a new HRIS/TMS/HCM or performance management standalone software. Contemporary TMSs and other emerging technologies support the new PM approach and can capture the appropriate feedback and development inputs and outputs in report or dashboard form.[156] Whether your organization chooses to invest in a TMS or a standalone PM system, technology can provide the foundation for implementing an updated performance management approach.

Some performance management tools include (but are not limited to)

- Personality and team profile tools designed to understand team dynamics and improve team dynamics and relationships;
- Financial and other tangible reward tools to motivate or demonstrate appreciation;
- Compensation management tools to reinforce rewards based on merit;
- Performance review forms and templates online to provide and archive formal written feedback;
- Competencies and skills matrices for staffing and individual performance information;[157]
- Coaching apps to provide guidance, give feedback on progress, and address issues;[158]
- Manager advice tools to assist managers in the feedback process;[159]
- Continuous feedback performance support online and mobile tools to provide feedback prompts that motivate or correct employees as part of the ongoing coaching process;[160] and
- Pulse surveys to request and receive feedback, gain insight into team inner workings, and compare to other teams—data can be aggregated and analyzed for immediate knowledge.[161]

Of course, no one is suggesting that the tools are the answer. However, behind the tools is a new philosophy of performance management. If your organization chooses to select an HR system that has a performance management module, it is important to know what PM methods your organization endorses in order to determine the requirements for the HR system. (See Chapter 9 for HR systems typology and those systems incorporating performance management modules.)

• • • • • • • • • •
CASE STUDY

Global Conglomerate Redesigning Its Performance Management Approach

A multinational conglomerate was known for its almost brutal use of the ranking performance management approach. Managers and staff viewed the process as subjective, demotivating, and uninstructive, but there seemed to be no alternatives. Within the organization, jobs were becoming more sophisticated, requiring problem-solving skills and independent judgment while demanding increased responsibilities. Customer relations were also becoming more complex. And yet the way of assessing the employees was not adapting to the times. The organization used performance scores as the basis for compensation. If you were ranked on the lower end of the bell curve, you were fired. Managers began showing increasing amounts of frustration and dissatisfaction over this approach, especially as a newer breed of hires appeared who were less competitive and not willing to stick around for the slaughter. But the possibility of replacing the existing system of performance review was daunting. What should replace it?

The bold decision was made to drop ratings, rankings, and annual reviews. The organization designed a new performance management system that was custom-made in-house. The new system includes a process that connects the company's performance objectives and the individual objectives so the individual objectives include prompts for updates as the company's objectives change. Further, the focus of evaluation is on the impact the team has on driving toward overall business goals. Archival information about long-term performance trends for teams is also tracked.

A tool is used to collect feedback and keep a record of when it is received. The tool also changes the tone and language of the feedback with coaching prompts that emphasize employee development rather than criticism by the manager delivering the feedback. The performance management tool gathers both quantitative and qualitative information that is available to the employee for viewing. Built into the tool is the capability to crowdsource feedback from peers and managers, either formally after a specific business milestone, or unprompted. This is done using an online mobile app that collects feedback in real time. Performance discussions focus on the input from this and other tools. By design, the performance conversations are more frequent, fact-based, and developmental. A new set of metrics is used to measure the performance of the team.

The jury is still out regarding the success of the new performance appraisal process, but some results are clear. The focus has shifted from interpersonal competition to open discussions and collaboration. There is a rise in employee-driven communication. The use of qualitative measures over rankings and the focus on performance development rather than appraisal helps employees be more responsive to customers through speed and collaboration. This approach is slowly changing the PM culture of the organization. The result is that the conglomerate is experiencing clear and impressive improvements in "employee engagement, time to market, and speed of innovation."[162]

MOBILE AUDIENCE RESPONSE POLLING SYSTEMS

As business professionals we may find ourselves managing or presenting policies in person to large groups of people. For instance, town halls have become widely used in both virtual and face-to-face formats. One way to gather feedback in face-to-face venues such as workgroups, conferences, and training classrooms is through using audience response systems.

A key trait common to highly regarded public speakers and instructors is their ability to engage the audience, keeping them alert, focused, and involved. One method for generating audience engagement is to provide interesting sessions, creative activities, and open discussions that encourage all to participate. Mobile audience response systems, such as Presentain (http://presentain.com/) and Poll Everywhere (https://www.polleverywhere.com/mobile), use technology to involve the audience. These response systems allow the speaker to pose questions to which participants respond using the texting feature on their cell phones. Questions typically are opinion polls. The polling software tabulates the data in real time and presents the results in a variety of formats, including charts, graphs, cloud, and text representation. Presentain allows participants to capture slides in the presentation, and the presenter can retain the audio record of the presentation as well as all the questions posted and the polling data. These polling devices rely on a technology most people carry with them—their mobile phones—and create an interactive environment in situations where audiences are typically passive. The software aggregates the audience's responses in a variety of formats (dashboard, charts, chat, etc.) viewable in the presentation software.

Another approach to audience feedback is a wireless response system that allows instructors to pose a question to which students respond by using a handheld response pad (called a clicker) to send information to a receiver. For a few examples, see iClicker or the Option Technologies audience response tools (https://www.optiontechnologies.com/audience-response-keypads). The advantage is that learners can answer multiple choice, true-false, yes-no, or survey-style questions presented to the class by the instructor.

Building a case for this response system is not difficult. The training needs for the presenter are minimal and very little instruction is necessary for trainees to begin using the system. All feedback gathered can be analyzed for patterns. This results in valuable knowledge that can inform decision-making.

SURVEYS AND QUESTIONNAIRES

Often HR professionals use surveys for collecting feedback and evaluation data. Donald Dillman, a leader in online survey development, provides insight into how to design an effective survey instrument for administration over the Internet. Dillman emphasizes a tailored design approach. This includes customizing the survey to the audience, encouraging survey response by giving "attention to all aspects of contacting and communicating with people," and developing a survey that builds positive social exchange.[163] This is easier said than done with what he calls the "dizzying array" of media available. The rule of thumb for selecting survey media is this: select the survey delivery instrument best suited to the audience and how they do their work.

Surveys can be designed using a free online tool (such as Survey Monkey, Typeform, Google Forms, or Client Heartbeat). They may be offered through another system, such as groupware like GoToMeeting or Collaborate Ultra at the end of a presentation, or they may be delivered by email. Surveys for training courseware, such as the end-of-course evaluation, may be embedded in the LCMS. The powerful aspect of this tool is that in many cases the advanced data analytics capabilities are built into the software and analysis results are immediately available.

Online survey tools typically have reporting capabilities. Survey reports can be produced in a variety of forms, including tables and charts. It is particularly important to be able to customize the reports to gather the best data. Be aware that some free online survey tools do not have the database and report-generating capabilities.

The emphasis on employee engagement gave rise to the design and issuance of the employee engagement survey, or the voice-of-the-employee survey. Perhaps one of the most expansive surveys conducted anywhere is the US government's Federal Employee Viewpoint (FedView) survey designed by the Office of Personnel Management (OPM). FedView "is a tool that measures employees' perceptions of whether, and to what extent, conditions characterizing successful organizations are present in their agencies. Survey results provide valuable insight into the challenges agency leaders face in ensuring the Federal Government has an effective civilian workforce and how well they are responding."[164] The FedView is conducted each year by OPM and the results for the past years are posted on a website for public viewing. Each agency can then get its own customized infogram highlighting standard categories including employee engagement. Some agencies follow the best practice of reporting the results and stating proposed actions to address any issues. Before the next survey, the agency communicates to its employees actions taken to rectify the issue(s).

A number of innovative and user-friendly feedback and evaluation devices exist. Evaluation takes many forms and serves a variety of purposes. Technology can be used to provide immediate feedback, ranging from performance evaluation to audience response polls to employee level-of-engagement surveys. Feedback and evaluation can be enabled and enhanced using cloud-based mobile programs to gather big data that can be analyzed and aggregated in visual form, as in dashboards with charts and graphs. The instruments and tools discussed in this chapter should help the HR manager find new, unique, and cost-effective methods to gather important and useful performance feedback. The results of evaluation and feedback when analyzed become important knowledge assets to be stored, shared, and used in decision making.

End-of-Chapter Technology Strategy Questions

Considering your organization's overall technology strategy, your HR technology strategy, and needs of your employees, answer the following:

1. How could performance management in your organization be improved, and how could technology be used in support of those proposed changes?
2. How does your organization gather employee engagement information? How could technology improve that process and how could the results be incorporated into knowledge management?
3. How should your organization's feedback and evaluation methods impact its HR technology strategy?

Digging Deeper

Berger, Lance A., and Dorothy R. Berger. 2017. *The Talent Management Handbook: Making Culture a Competitive Advantage by Acquiring, Identifying, Developing, and Promoting the Best People*. 3rd ed. New York: McGraw Hill.

Dessler, Gary, and Biju Varkkey. 2016. *Human Resource Management*. 14th ed. Noida, Ind.: Pearson.

CHAPTER 15

Social Networks

TOPICS COVERED IN THIS CHAPTER

- What are social networks?

- Social networks and knowledge management

- Organizational benefits of social networks

- Social networks, the portal, and mobile devices

- A case for social networking

- Potential disadvantages of social networks

- Legal considerations for social network use

Social networks first appeared as a nonbusiness application, but they have found a place in the business realm. Business applications of social networks flourish. As mentioned in Chapter 2, social networking and social media represent trending technologies for the HR profession. We will start with a differentiation between social networks and social media. Then the benefits and business applications appear. Standards for use in the workplace and legal considerations follow. Along the way, you will see examples of organizations effectively using social networking. Consider how social networking could align with and enhance your organization's HR strategy.

WHAT ARE SOCIAL NETWORKS?

Social networks refer to the online clustering of individuals into groups, like small rural communities or a neighborhood subdivision. Social networks provide a simulated version of the in-person networking environment with all of the associated professional and personal benefits.

The Internet is filled with millions of individuals who are looking to meet other like-minded people. Social network services (SNSs) connect individuals with similar interests regardless of their geographical locations. The topics and interests exchanged on social networks are varied and rich. The term "social networking sites" also appears in public discourse and is often used interchangeably with social media. To narrow the scope of this chapter and preserve the early definition of social networks, we will maintain a distinction between the two.

Different categories of social networks exist. Facebook is a social net-working website where you can create profiles, exchange private or public messages, join with friends, make new friends, and so on. It is used by many as a personal space. LinkedIn is considered by many to be a business social network, but neither service is limited to one context or the other. LinkedIn has risen to preeminence because of its powerful grip on the business community. Twitter is also a social network. Although the for-profit world has not embraced Twitter as its network of choice, in the social and, more recently, political realms, Twitter is very influential. Even YouTube can be considered a social network.

On any social network site, users create a profile and then interact with other users, creating new relationships and maintaining existing ones. Some organizations run effective online marketing campaigns within their social networks. Since everyone has their favorite social networks, rather than create a list, we ask that you consider the social network you use most often as the basis for this definition.

A common for-profit use for SNSs is marketing through advertisements. Sourcing potential candidates for a certain job position is another. Politicians use social network sites to identify and attract voters. Organizations use SNSs to stay connected with other associated businesses. Social networks are also used for building CoPs and affinity groups, and for learning. The unique learning aspect of social networks is the opportunity to access resources, information, subject matter experts, and discussions with those of differing opinions whom you may never meet or have access to in your normal dealings.[165] There are many business uses for SNSs.

Social networks rely on a variety of tools embedded in the service itself with the goal of connecting people. Interaction occurs through the use of email, blogs, instant messages, text, podcasts, photographs, and video for social, professional, and business purposes. The goal of a social network is to build trust and knowledge assets within a specific community.

Tony Bingham and Marcia Conner consider social networks as a force creating a radical shift in the way we learn. The authors offer a variety of trends that set the scene for using social networks for learning at work. They point out four major trends that are shifting the way we work:

1. The accelerated pace of change requires agility;
2. Technology goes where we go without boundaries (mobile);
3. Shifting workplace demographics alter expectations; and
4. People desire personal connection.

All four of these serve as the impetus for increased use of social networks and, in their view, social learning.[166] They also set the scene for the use of social networks at work.

SOCIAL NETWORKS AND KNOWLEDGE MANAGEMENT

When social networks began, they tended to be used for sharing photos, videos, and gossip. However, social networks have grown into a mainstream business tool. Social networks have a variety of applications that are valuable to organizations. These applications have been widely touted in support of social networks and they are only increasing in number. Organizations may also create their own organization-based social networks:

- **Informational social networks.** Informational communities are made up of people seeking answers to everyday problems.
- **Professional social networks.** Participants use these to advance within their career.
- **Academic social networks.** ARPANET, the US Department of Defense's original network, is used for collaboration within the scientific community.
- **Training and development social networks.** Learners participate with others in order to make sense of new ideas in training and development.
- **News related social networks.** Contain "community content" where members are allowed to make comments, post news stories, or anything else.

ORGANIZATIONAL BENEFITS OF SOCIAL NETWORKS

The social network has completely changed the way people interact. With a tool that powerful and undeniably appealing, that engages millions of people in one place, at one time, with common interests—organizations need to understand it and join in the conversation.

Social networks can be used for strategic planning. Organizations may use social networks to create contacts among employees, form teams, or staff new projects. They are also valuable for staffing unique skill sets. Recruiting, organizational branding for marketing, and building customer relationships can be done using social networks.

For knowledge management purposes, social networks can be used to connect employees and facilitate information sharing or knowledge transfer. Some organizations use the social network to blog and generate innovative ideas, which can be captured and shared through the KM system. Most organizations are using social networks to make information accessible, in which case you could call the social network a knowledge-sharing network.[167]

Social networks can also be used to find translators for transactions with customers who speak other languages, as substitutes for internal emails, and to connect new hires during onboarding with other new hires, mentors, managers, and team members.[168] Dialoging about common issues and innovative ideas and sharing documents between project team members or others within the organization are also positive uses for social networks.

SOCIAL NETWORKS, THE PORTAL, AND MOBILE DEVICES

Interestingly, many organizations are turning to their portals to enable social networks (see Chapter 11 for information about portals). The advantage of the Facebook-like directories available through the portal and internal social network sites is that employees can share expertise, join CoPs, or simply connect with each other. The advantage is that the internal social network is more private and organization specific, and can be controlled by the organization to some extent.

Cloud and mobile social networks harness and disseminate information. Social networks are becoming a personal job agent that captures an individuals' digital footprint and exhibits their profile on the web. Mobile access to social networks through the cloud easily facilitates the network's power. The mobile computing aspect contributes to the workforce trend toward job hopping. Conducting business using mobile social networks enables individuals to constantly be looking for new opportunities online.[169]

With regard to the propensity to job hop, technology companies such as TalentBin by Monster, Entel, RemarkableHire, and Gild can track an individual's social history to evaluate them as a candidate.[170] They can then mine that candidate's online social information to create a profile. These are particularly helpful programs for companies with open positions in hard-to-fill areas. Social networking communities also become feeding grounds for e-recruiting, talent hunters who leverage the communities where talent congregates in order to identify new hire prospects.

Mobile sourcing hinges on social networking. Since most adults in the United States have mobile phones, mobile social networking is the primary platform for job candidates and organizations. The obvious advantage is that organizations that adopt a mobile-optimized career site put themselves in an advantageous position.

TIPS AND TOOLS FOR SOCIAL NETWORKS

- Examine the social network use and policies of other organizations in your industry.
- Determine whether social networks can benefit your organization.
- Identify whether there is an organizational policy regarding the use of social networks on the job.
- Use best practices to create a policy statement for employee use of social networks.
- Draft a business case in support of an organizational implementation of a social network, if it is appropriate for your organization.
- Communicate the organizational policy toward social networks at an organizational level and at the individual employee level.

A CASE FOR SOCIAL NETWORKING

Financial services organizations typically resist the allure of technology. There are many compliance challenges that hamper the use of cloud-based tools and add extra complexity to technology innovations. One financial agency, however, decided to break out of the mold. This financial services organization (FSO) started a digital journey into employee social networks using Yammer. For this organization the challenge was to create a cultural change that embraced the new digital tools. Thankfully there was a real appetite for social and mobile collaboration, making the cultural shift easier to navigate. The goal was to create digital and social capability in order to provide the cultural context for use of other new tools.

The organization chose to follow best practices to implement the new social network. First, the HR department created a vision for the digital workspace. Second, they ensured compliance with all legal restraints to cloud-based technologies. The goals were to make the social network—in this case Yammer— an extension of accepted communication channels. Third, video case studies were used to engage the employees and a request for stakeholders was issued. There was an overwhelming response to the latter, an indication of organizational readiness for the new technology. Fourth, the FSO created a pilot for Yammer. Then, fifth, using Yammer as a tool to shift the culture toward a different working paradigm, there was a campaign to enroll people in Yammer. The goal was to portray digital technology as an enabler of business behaviors like collaboration and innovation for the end goal of building a social culture where employees are empowered to participate in the digital workspace.

Yammer guidelines for feedback and collaboration included the following:

- Encourage employees to discuss news and issues.
- Crowdsource information to get answers to questions.
- Get the word out by posting answers to annoying technology problems and frequently asked technology questions.
- Generate conversations by offering information only available through Yammer.
- Connect people.
- Be professional, sensible, polite, and constructive.

The result of this effort is that the Yammer pilot membership includes over one-third of the organization, and that number is growing. Ultimately, the organization inculcated Yammer into their digital channels. The pilot was very successful and engagement persists as people use Yammer for unique, creative business applications. For-profit, government, and nonprofit organizations are instituting similar programs with equal success.

POTENTIAL DISADVANTAGES OF SOCIAL NETWORKS

There are some perceived—and real—disadvantages to social networks. Employers are concerned that employees visiting social sites while working will result in lower productivity or lead some to jeopardize corporate data. Further, there are risks of identity theft for those who use social networks. Users are prompted to provide personal information, and every bit of personal information that an identity thief obtains can be used to fill in the blanks and possibly steal an identity.

Employers are using social networks to review and vet potential hires, even though that practice may have legal implications from a discrimination standpoint: "Companies must take care not to allow the person making the hiring decision to become aware of a candidate's political or religious views–or any other information that could lead to a claim of hiring discrimination. For this reason, some employers opt to use third-party services for scanning social media sites or otherwise separate any social media scanning from any hiring manager's duties."[171] Further, not every candidate uses social networking, so they could complain that organizations that depend on vetting and or sourcing based on social network presence as a prerequisite are discriminatory.

Some social networks' privacy settings have shortcomings. Facebook tells its users that they (the users) have control over their personal information and who sees it; however, the site does occasionally update itself, which may disrupt individual privacy settings, so it behooves users to periodically review their privacy settings. Facebook has basic visibility rules that allow friends and people in network to see a user's profile, but social networkers should be cautious regarding protecting their online privacy.

It is a bit of a bind. Having your privacy set to the absolute lowest visibility to those outside the immediate network could impede the very interactions that social networkers seek. However, that information can also be misused. Until such time that clear mandates are established, common sense dictates that both individuals and businesses err on the side of caution in their use of social networking sites and what they post on these sites.

Finally, at the time of this writing, two social networks are coming under fire for their lack of controls over what are perceived as antisocial and dangerous elements. At least one global firm plans to withdraw ads from social networking sites "that do not protect our children or which create division in society, and promote anger or hate."[172] This introduces the topic that some social networks are more appropriate for business purposes than others.[173] This is a determination that your organization will make based on its mission and vision, but one that HR must be aware of and consider.

LEGAL CONSIDERATIONS FOR SOCIAL NETWORK USE

The laws regarding social network use, like those regarding the use of some other new technologies, are having trouble keeping up with the technology. An excellent article in *HR Magazine* provides some tips for using social networks for vetting applicants: Check social media later in the vetting process, be consistent (either check the social networking profiles for every potential hire or do not check any of them; avoid picking and choosing whose profiles you examine), document your decisions and print out the social media page that influenced consideration, and look at the candidate's posts and not those of another person posting on the candidate's site.

As social networking becomes more pervasive, so does the range of influence of comments posted on social network sites. Employers must avoid any comments or posts about an employee as it could go viral. On the flip side, increasingly employees are using social media to post negative comments about organizations and coworkers. With regard to defamatory comments toward employees or from an employee toward the organization, this is the present status: "While defamatory comments are not illegal, the law does protect employers when an employee harasses or defames a co-worker and that coworker sues the employer for failing to prevent such harassment. Likewise, Employment Practices Liability Insurance will protect the employer when a manager is responsible for the inappropriate post, tweet, or tag."[174]

The rule of thumb when using social networking sites internal to your organization is to consider the laws of the land where the organization is headquartered. In the United States, it is important to examine state laws as well federal laws when writing policy. In cases of disparity between laws, comply with the most stringent. Unfortunately, as new technologies emerge or increase in sophistication, there are cases where the law has not kept pace. In these cases, organizational policies should anticipate potential issues. The employee's required behavior becomes a matter of ethics and etiquette. As stated above, HR professionals must encourage their organizations to provide clear and comprehensive policies regarding employee use of technologies on the job.

Social networks provide valuable services when used appropriately in the workplace. Common uses for SNSs include marketing, communicating, reviewing applicant credentials, building communities of learning, and training. There are many different types of social networks, and they serve different purposes. New applications for SNSs continue to emerge. Since the laws have not kept pace with this technology, if your organization is using SNSs, be sure to institute a policy regarding acceptable and unacceptable uses for social networks in the workplace.

End-of-Chapter Technology Strategy Questions

Considering your organization's overall business strategy, the technology strategy of your HR department, and the needs of your employees, answer the following:

1. How does your organization leverage the power of social networks for knowledge management purposes?
2. If social networking is not in the organization's repertoire, how might it be effectively implemented to extend the mission and purpose of your organization and enhance the overall HR technology strategy?

Digging Deeper

Bingham, Tony, and Marcia Conner. 2015. *The New Social Learning: Connect. Collaborate. Work.* Alexandria: ATD Press.

Isson, Jean Paul, and Jesse S. Herriott. 2016. *People Analytics in the Era of Big Data: Changing the Way You Attract, Acquire, Develop, and Retain Talent.* Hoboken, NJ: Wiley and Sons.

CHAPTER 16

HR as a Strategic Partner

TOPICS COVERED IN THIS CHAPTER

- Technology, leadership, and HR business partners (HRBPs)

- HRBPs as change agents

- HR metrics

- Digital disruption in the cognitive era

- Evolution of talent acquisition—the case for cognitive talent acquisition at IBM today

TECHNOLOGY, LEADERSHIP, AND HR STRATEGIC BUSINESS PARTNERS (HRBPS)

The last five years have brought a massive alteration to the HR profession. Events and technologies pushed HR out of a predominantly background administrative role into the limelight. Suddenly, the HR department has become critical to the success of organizations and, as such, a strategic partner. This radical change caught many HR professionals by surprise. Suddenly, HR has a preeminent role in decision. What caused this (welcome) change? Some would say that it has to do with technology, as the new HR systems offer previously unattainable capabilities in reporting, managing, decision support, and providing logical, streamlined alternatives to aging and outdated HR practices.

The important thing to remember is that time stands still for no person. Those HR professionals who understand HR technologies and trends as well as their uses will be at the forefront of this transition, leading the way. They will be able to collaborate with other department leaders and understand the performance metrics and analytic tools used to examine and draw conclusions from HR data. Further, they will contribute to their organization's intangibles, such as customer service, ethics, and social responsibility. They will communicate effectively with stakeholders throughout the organization and will experience the rush of leading the charge successfully.

In contrast, the HR professionals who choose to hold tightly to the way things were will find themselves at the mercy of other people's decisions, using systems they don't understand, being required to perform tasks for which they do not have the skills, and struggling to keep up.

The new HR role focuses on workforce management, virtual teams, performance management, employee engagement, globalization, and management development, all of which are enhanced through constructive use of technology. Since HR professionals typically already possess change management and communication skills, those will be repurposed for consulting with other internal departments and building collaborative relationships. In this chapter we will point out several areas where the adaptive and agile HR professional can have a positive impact.

HR BUSINESS PARTNERS AS CHANGE AGENTS

In the book *HR Business Partners*, Hunter et al. set the scene for how this change in the HR role will take place. The model in *HR Business Partners* portrays HR in a more consultative role with clearly defined skills.[175] As consultants, we are relating and engaging with managers by viewing them as clients, talking their language, networking, and sharing ideas across functions. We must diagnose organizational conditions by connecting the business strategy to the role of HR, understanding workplace issues, using analytical skills to challenge the client's thinking, and staying current with external trends that should be incorporated into the HR strategy. We are intervening to shape the change agenda rather than reacting to it, proactively responding to anticipated people-management issues, making recommendations, determining obstacles to change, and identifying ways to overcome them.

As change agents, we contract with business partners to explain the benefits of change, use project management approaches with clients, ensure standards are clear, and find the resources and appropriate people to deliver projects. We deliver the promised outputs, coach others in change tools and techniques, communicate appropriately, and identify risks and their benefits. We know how to evaluate performance using clear milestones, metrics, and benchmarks, and examine outputs as well as lessons learned from successes and failures.[176]

HR professionals have the skills needed to add value and positively impact business outcomes. Clearly, however, these roles and responsibilities cannot be done alone, so HR professionals must be team players, sharing knowledge, grooming talent, and participating in initiatives that contribute to the success of the entire organization. We must lead by example.

John Kotter talks about leading change in his book by that name. Leading change requires superb relational skills, including emotional intelligence, which is considered more important to effective management than any technical skill.[177] Leading change also requires the ability to develop and communicate a strategy that incorporates short-term wins and builds momentum via incremental changes within the organizational culture.[178]

HR METRICS

Measurements for HR performance are pretty straightforward (days to hire, number of adverse incidences, performance data showing top performers, employee retention, etc.), but determining how to gather that information is more complicated. HR professionals must contribute in a way that is valuable and significant in measurable terms to the organization. HR is most effective by furthering the objectives of their internal business partners. The business units and organizational goals and objectives will help HR determine what information to gather.

The HR literature tells us there are three categories of analytics: HR metrics, organization capability, and talent. Foundational HR metrics can be expressed in numbers such as completed initiatives, percentages, or cost benefits. Valuable business information to which HR is privy could be the percentage of disabled veterans employed, or the percentage of the total workforce on the verge of retiring within an organization. The cost-benefit information relevant to HR metrics might be cost of hiring, expenses per employee, and technical training costs (versus financial losses due to errors). HR analytics are enabled by reliable data, which can come from integrated systems or a single system handling all of the HR functions involved in gathering the data.

Improving Business Processes

As change agents, HR professionals should anticipate the impact of disruptive technologies, and assist in the redefinition of an organization's business processes. This is best understood by using the opposite for comparison. An HR professional who is not a change agent waits for things to happen and then scrambles to adjust. Improving business processes requires anticipation and awareness of the trends both internal and external to the organization. There is no need to revisit the skills of business process reengineering as that is one of the competencies basic to HR. What *is* new are the processes of gathering information and predicting where the change will occur in order to mitigate potential disruption and pave the way for change. Clearly, organizations seeking to maximize employee engagement, process efficiencies, return on investment, and organization performance will need to embrace the new disruptive technologies and deal with the impact on business processes.

Business process reengineering will probably be necessary if a new HR technology strategy is implemented. It is the HR professional's responsibility to participate as a partner in the "as-is" and "to-be" analyses and mitigate negative impact (see Chapter 9). In managing these aspects of a new HR technology introduction, the HR professional significantly contributes to the organization at a strategic level in applying these analyses.

Building Relationships

Improving HR business processes and business processes impacted by new HR systems is a responsibility that is dependent on gathering external data not only through boundary spanning and collaboration, but also through the relationships built with the internal clients. HR must not be relegated to its bubble to make policies and arrange awards banquets. The pace and complexity of change in technology alone requires constant vigilance. No one can read enough or study enough to stay abreast of the changes occurring in technology and its impact on organizations. If HR maintains relationships with the internal customer and ongoing communication within external CoPs, it is less likely to get sideswiped by emerging required competencies and technologies.

The workplace today relies on collaboration among people working in different offices, sometimes continents apart, and also those who are working remotely, away from an office environment completely. Virtual teams are now commonplace. It is important for the HR leader to create an environment that cultivates collaboration and builds relationships. By partnering with team leaders, the HR professional can assist with recommendations that facilitate team collaboration. More importantly, HR can assist teams with developing online protocols and standards as well as team norms so that the virtual teams function in a healthy, productive manner.

Fostering Individual Growth

Global workforce cultural shifts offer challenges to virtual teamwork and technology adaptation. The multicultural workforce is growing and international outsourcing is increasing as well. Together these two events have had a dramatic impact on communication and cultural norms. Sometimes these forces create conflict. However, these workforce dynamics and stressors can be mitigated when HR professionals help team members establish working practices that support communication and respect cultural differences. When the conflict results from outsourcing, the organizational policy and reasoning should be clearly communicated through HR. In fact, the HR professional should provide a communication conduit to the employees they serve.

Diverse workplace demographics result in a variety of reactions especially when introducing new technologies. These expectations are not inherently good nor bad; they simply require flexibility and innovation on the part of HR professionals to address potential resistance. If expectations are met, the result can be dramatic shifts in workplace practices and policies. The HR professionals must be flexible, responsive, and creative to maximize the ROI.

As mentioned earlier, in recent years, HR professionals have taken on a consultative, rather than administrative, role. As such, we must identify issues and assist managers in developing their problem-solving skills. Management development can occur in any number of ways, including training. The goal, however, is for the HR professional to serve as a business partner. When developing managers through instruction, coaching, or mentoring professionals must use the technology insights gleaned from this text to facilitate these relationships and processes.

Generating Employee Engagement

Many confuse measuring employee engagement with promoting it. We have learned that engaged employees make for a more productive workplace. To quote Dessler and Varkkey, some ways to increase employee engagement include making sure employees understand how their departments contribute to the company's success, see how their own efforts contribute to achieving the company's goals, and get a sense of accomplishment from working at the firm.[179]

If you are working in an environment where many of the employees are not involved and enthusiastic, you are likely positioned to be the change agent who seeks to identify the source of the problem and influence, in a positive way, the workplace culture. Keep in mind that a toxic environment can occur when workers do not have the proper tools to do their jobs. In such cases, the HR technology strategy may contribute to the solution.

Collaborating with Business Partners as Customers

Internally, HR leaders can communicate new ideas and improve collaboration between business units by championing CoPs and CoLs (communities of learning). Both require mutual engagement, a joint enterprise, and a shared repertoire of practices. CoPs typically refer to groups of practitioners that newcomers enter and attempt to learn the cultural ways. A CoL, on the other hand, is a group of people who, while sharing common values and beliefs, actively engage in learning from each other. Led by HR professionals, both CoPs and CoLs can be used to enable the exchange of ideas and collaborative learning.

Technology can connect people and encourage formation of CoPs and CoLs. Social media tools like microblogs, chat, YouTube, wikis, and podcasts can assist the HR professional in building CoPs/CoLs and help an employees communicate across business units in an efficient manner. Additionally, social networks and groupware represent tools that can facilitate communication and community.

Dealing with Intangibles

As globalization increases, intangibles (such as risk-taking, integrity, customer service, innovation, and social responsibility) change. *Globalization*, simply described, is the process by which national and regional economies, societies, and cultures have become integrated through a global network supported by communication, transportation, and trade. The globalization of organizations as it exists today was made possible by technology. Corporations recognized the potential power and benefits of being able to be both centralized (in structure) and decentralized (in geography) for years, but could not put the theory into practice until the needed technologies emerged.

Globalization highlights the need for social responsibility. We, as HR professionals, should care not only about the organization's success in a global economy, but also about the other cultures and people who are touched by the organization. As we gain technical competence, we should give back. A consideration for global organizations is how to be socially responsible and benefit the communities in which we operate. Corporate social responsibility builds employee engagement when people are focused on something bigger than themselves. In global organizations, the HR professional should be the change agent who spearheads the discussion about social responsibility as an intangible, yet critical, contribution.

Leading Change by Introducing Appropriate Technologies

Not every organization is at the leading edge of technology. A variety of conditions can hold an organization back; however, even with things such as financial restrictions, customer expectations, lack of leadership vision, company culture, perceived expense of HR technology investments, and the like, there is no need for HR to lag behind. HR should be leading the charge toward thinking of new and creative ways to leverage technology to the benefit of the organization and its employees. The true HRBP seeks to promote the organization's mission and vision and doing so in a cost effective way. HR can contribute to cost efficiencies, streamline communication, knowledge management, and employee engagement by designing and implementing an HR technology strategy that enhances organizational performance. That is HR's role as strategic business partner.

Nevertheless, leadership is not for the faint of heart. You will need emotional intelligence that prevents you from reaction and defensiveness. Servant leadership fits well to this form of guiding others. Servant leaders conceptualize creative solutions to multifaceted problems with a thorough understanding of the organization. Humility and a desire to promote the well-being of another are at the core of servant leadership. Servant leaders are sensitive to the personal concerns, well-being, and aspirations of others and make themselves available. They help others grow and succeed by making their career development a priority and using tools such as mentoring and coaching to provide support. Servant leaders behave ethically and create value for the workplace. They empower others to be independent—not dependent—and in so doing promote self-sufficiency.[180] How does leadership of this type relate to technology and change? Since technology is in a constant state of flux and the workplace adapts in order to stay current, it takes a strong sense of self and an ability to lead change efforts to enable others to do their best. The HR professional must be an anchor amid technology's undulating trends.

TIPS AND TOOLS FOR BEING AN HR BUSINESS PARTNER

- Grow your understanding of HR technologies, business, practices, HR-relevant metrics, and Return on Investment (ROI).

- Use systems, queries, and analytics to examine relevant data for patterns and trends.

- Assist with cross-division communication through appropriate technology use to eliminate organizational silos and encourage collaboration.

- Seek to create improved business processes and document those that already exist.

- Foster relationships throughout the organization and use technology to assist others to do so.

- Set up business processes and design training and select technologies that will improve and support employee performance.

- Be proactive in dealing with intangibles such as customer service, ethics, and sustainability.

- Join an HR community of practice such as SHRM (www.shrm.org), Association for Talent Development (ATD; www.td.org), the Academy of Human Resource Development (AHRD; www.ahrd.org), HR People + Strategy (HRPS; www.hrps.org), or the International Society for Performance Improvement (ISPI; www.ispi.org).

DIGITAL DISRUPTION IN THE COGNITIVE ERA

We are at the forefront of digital transformation, where software is impacting social change through machines that can talk, see, understand, reason, answer questions, and even help recruit candidates. Through artificial intelligence, or what IBM refers to as cognitive computing, disruption is occurring across industries at a much faster pace than ever before. While some companies are already advanced in consuming and managing data—the currency of the new digital and cognitive era—many will need to transform and integrate technology to gather greater insights. As you can imagine, this transformation is not an easy task nor one that can be solved by technology alone. Given that it affects culture, structure, common processes, and people—with a host of implications for talent—HR is at the heart of this digital and cognitive transformation using consulting, strategizing, and change agent skills to ease the transition. In fact, organizational lines of business are eager for HR to step up as a strategic partner. The next case demonstrates how HR visionaries can leverage leading-edge technology and positively impact talent acquisition to benefit an entire organization including all of their business partners.

•••••••••••
CASE STUDY

Evolution of Talent Acquisition: The Case for Cognitive Talent Acquisition at IBM Today

Dr. Robert Gibby and Emily Herbert

As an illustration of the important roles digital and cognitive technology are playing in HR, consider the technological evolution of talent acquisition over the past forty years. Staffing emerged in the 1980s with the advent of ATSs and evolved into recruitment by leveraging job boards like Monster and CareerBuilder in the 1990s. It then transitioned to talent acquisition in the mid-2000s through leveraging social solutions like LinkedIn, Twitter, and YouTube. Over the next decade, talent acquisition incorporated digital technologies to engage candidates to win the "war for talent." Today, it's clear the war for talent has been won by candidates. Now, organizations are engaged in a "fight for fit" to attract the right talent, at the right time, for the right job. It is in this fight that cognitive solutions will become paramount in the successful transformation of talent acquisition.

With Watson, IBM is leading the development of cognitive computing solutions that allow us to identify talent with greater speed and predictability while providing a more engaging candidate experience. In 2015, we launched Find Your Fit—a cognitive solution that matched candidates to best-fit jobs based solely on their résumés. It worked by combining natural language, machine learning, and other cognitive services from Watson to extract concepts from the résumé and job profile, match these concepts, and ultimately, identify best-fit jobs.

From this foundation, we have expanded the solution to create a candidate assistant that engages candidates in deeper conversation about the company and recommends jobs relevant to a candidate's background, skills, and interests. Watson learns about the candidate through a series of text-based natural conversations and responds in real time to their questions about IBM (e.g., our culture, benefits, work locations) just like a recruiter would. Through mid-2017, more than fifty thousand candidates have been assisted by Watson, with 93 percent reviewing job recommendations and 35 percent applying to a job. As a testament to the more engaging experience, we increased our candidate net promoter score by 41 points from our Find Your Fit baseline. We also learned what candidates want to know about IBM through their questions, aiding our ability to develop branding stories that better engage our candidates via social channels and IBM meet-up events.

IBM is also working to replace traditional assessments (e.g., personality and cognitive ability tests) with new video assessment and game experiences built with AI and machine learning. As an example, a 2017 pilot of a new problem-solving game resulted in equivalent or better prediction to our traditional cognitive ability test, a total lack of bias in prediction, and a 3:1 preference among test takers—all in an experience that takes a quarter of the time to complete compared to the traditional test.

Moving forward, we will continue to leverage cognitive computing to provide a more personalized and engaging candidate experience independent of whether they end up becoming an IBMer. For those who are offered jobs, we will leverage cognitive computing to provide personalized offer packages that candidates can further tweak to fit their needs. We will also strive to achieve things never thought possible in the talent acquisition function.

Moving beyond assisting the candidate, we are now engaged in training Watson to provide decision support to recruiters and hiring managers via a rank-ordered list of active candidates scored on their likelihood to be successful at a particular job. To help win in the fight for fit, we will expand this predictive capability to evaluating passive candidates, enabling recruiters to engage and convert best-fit candidate leads who aren't looking for a new job. Watson will also help us transform how we interview by guiding the formation of optimal interview panels, suggesting relevant interview questions, and ultimately, listening to candidate responses to provide provisional rating recommendations to the interviewer.

As illustrated in these examples, data—and increasingly unstructured data—are fueling the digital disruption happening in the Talent Acquisition industry. The cognitive solutions we are developing and training at IBM operate on this formerly invisible data in new ways to provide augmented intelligence to candidates, recruiters, and hiring managers (HR Business Partners) to help ensure the right fit exists before a candidate becomes an employee. Successful cognitive solutions will provide intelligence that is inclusive of diversity, engaging, and personalized to the decision maker. IBM Talent Acquisition is confident the solutions outlined above, along with new ones we dream up, will help to transform how people find their dream jobs and how next-generation recruiters can attract the right fits for their organization.

Robert E. Gibby, PhD, Chief Talent Scientist for IBM Talent Acquisition, leads a team of experts focused on creating cognitive computing (Watson), assessment, and analytics solutions that deliver quality hires through more engaging and personalized experiences. He was elected a Fellow of the Society for Industrial and Organizational Psychology in 2014 and has received multiple industry awards for his work, including the 2013 SHRM HR Impact Award.

Emily Herbert, MSc, Talent Scientist Market Focal for IBM Talent Acquisition, leads the design, development, and governance of next-generation cognitive computing (Watson), assessment, interview, and analytics solutions. As the Market Focal, she partners with regional and line leadership to drive impact and quality of hire in bringing these solutions to market. She is a Member of the British Psychological Society.

• • • • • • • • • • •

In this chapter, we examined the role of HR as a strategic business partner, essentially guiding the way toward business transformation made necessary by new HR technologies. HR Business Partners use metrics for decision making, improve business processes, build relationships, foster individual growth, generate employee engagement, communicate effectively, deal with intangibles, and lead change. The final case demonstrates how emerging technologies—such as cognitive talent acquisition—require a forward-looking strategy and why HR Business Partners must lead the charge.

End-of-Chapter Technology Strategy Questions

Considering your organization's overall business strategy and the role of the HR department, answer the following:

1. How does your organization perceive and implement the HR-as-business-partner role (or not)?
2. How could your HR department provide better service and HR technology support to the lines of business?
3. How is your organization responding to the disruptive technologies that are rocking HR (mobile, social media, data analytics, IoT, and cloud computing)?
4. What needed changes would you make to your organization's HR technology strategy to incorporate learning management, talent management and knowledge management and why?

Digging Deeper

Hunter, Ian, Jane Saunders, Allan Boroughs, and Simon Constance. 2016. *HR Business Partners.* 2nd ed. New York: Routledge.

Kotter, John P. 2012. *Leading Change.* Boston: Harvard Business Publishing.

CHAPTER 17

Future Trends for Technology and HR

Predictions about the field of human resource development (HRD) generally include an expanded role for technology. One cannot dismiss technology as an underpinning of HRD functions. In fact, a review of current articles about HR trends projects HR technology growth in all the major HR functional areas. We can conclude that HR technologies will continue to play a pivotal role in organizations. Consequently, HR managers—indeed, all HR professionals—must get on board. In the twenty-first century, *organizations that do not use technology effectively* to improve organizational, team, and individual performance will be left behind.

The common practice now—in order to keep pace with the trends impacting HR—is for consulting firms to provide yearly predictions. Books foretelling the future of HR and the HR department abound.[181] Further, technology and its impact on the workplace remain in the forefront of daily news. What follows are predictions that impact HR, grouped into three categories: the future workplace, HR technologies, and HR strategic thinking. Let's start with the workplace.

FUTURE WORKPLACE TRENDS

HR leaders should follow a few key workplace trends in order to be informed about and navigate the uncertainties of the future. Understanding these trends will allow HR to better prepare for their inevitable impact on the way people work. Using our leadership and change agent skills to anticipate and prepare for these trends will mitigate disruption and maximize benefits to the organization.

Boomerang Employees

Boomerang employees are those who leave and return. The acceptance of boomerang employees is a trend that will occur primarily because professionals are switching jobs more often. The benefits to an organization of rehiring employees are many, and include decreased onboarding costs and training requirements. Additionally, the returning employees will undoubtedly bring new perspectives and new knowledge. This contributes to the pool of knowledge in the knowledge management system. HR will need to change its standard recruiting and hiring approach to accommodate rehiring boomerang employees.

Shift in Leadership Styles

The leadership mantle will shift from "hero leaders" to high-performing teams, with some even hired and compensated as intact teams.[182] This swing toward team leadership will compel HR to evaluate performance differently. Specifically, HR will need to have the tools to assess how well the team works collectively to achieve organizational goals. Leaders within the team will also have to adjust leadership style to accommodate shared or distributed leadership. Team lead responsibilities will be to monitor and assist the team to ensure it succeeds.[183]

Agile Performance Feedback and Performance Support

The emphasis on and growth of work teams will require agile performance measures, check-ins, team-developed shared goals, and regular developmental conversations instead of the once-per-year session. Performance assessment must include employee-to-employee feedback, employee-to-manager feedback, and manager-to-employee feedback, which will occur through connected cloud platforms. As for performance support tools, they will look more like games than traditional checklists or performance aids.[184]

Gig Workers

Gig workers accomplish specific tasks and then leave. HR will have to adjust its benefits programs to accommodate gig workers for flexibility and to save money.[185] Some think that the future of gig workers is that they will team up to take on self-organized projects and leadership roles.[186] The challenges to HR will be compensation plans outside the normal model, the need for flexibility, how to handle accountability, benefits, and managing gig workers to name a few. In any case, the gig worker is here to stay.

Office Space Enhancing Office Culture

The design of office space will become more geared toward teamwork and less based on individual workspaces. Office space will change to provide open areas where teams can congregate. All the tools necessary for collaboration will need to be available in these group work areas. A further blurring of work and home life will occur as companies push to integrate workers even further into the workplace by creating a workplace experience that feels like home.

This will include ways to create a "second shift" of after-hours work that is supportive of home-life needs including concierge services, such as shopping, dinner arrangements, and dry cleaning pickup.[187] HR will have to adjust to these changes, arranging any private performance conversations purposefully because of the lack of private office spaces or specific office hours. This will also bring about a different way to evaluate work, deemphasizing the hours spent at work and emphasizing instead the results and impact.[188]

Power of Multiple Generations

Multigenerational and multicultural employee resource groups will have more strategic influence in the workplace.[189] HR needs to adjust to respect and promote employees' individuality and to reject bias based on any status (such as age, race, gender, religion, worldview) in all of its policies, writings, and even wording in recruitment ads.[190]

HR as a Business Partner and Workplace Activist

As mentioned in Chapters 1 and 2, the role of the HR professional is shifting. Going forward, HR professionals will become more of a business partner to the lines of business. This requires that HR learn the business inside and out, build great and diverse networks of relationships, be at the leading edge of business thinking, and develop as an employee champion capable of defining, tracking, reporting, and celebrating individual and business successes. As workplace activists, we have to rethink our role and move beyond our comfort zone to develop business acumen, then apply what we have learned from the business mindset to HR. "Your job is to help your organization win in an increasingly volatile, uncertain, complex, and ambiguous marketplace and HR is the catalyst to do this."[191]

Shared Service Centers (SSCs) and Centers of Excellence

Standardization, centralization, and technology enablement will occur in the SSCs. This consolidation will provide valuable information and feedback that will in turn impact policy-making. As a result, HR centers of excellence (CoEs) will emerge to define policy and provide oversight for the shared service center.[192]

FUTURE HR TECHNOLOGY TRENDS

Gartner, Forrester, McKinsey, Deloitte, SHRM, and others prognosticate about the future of HR technologies. Their predictions appear here and are grouped into the following categories: social media, mobile technology, data and analytics, cloud computing, MOOCs, IoT, AI, robotics, and blockchains.

Social Media

The social media technology is quickly becoming the technology of choice for organizations. A Gallup poll in 2015 indicated that 70 percent of American workers are not engaged in email and 30 percent of respondents said they ignore employer's emails.[193] This trend will only become more pronounced and will cause a shift in modes of communication from email to social media. Further, the increasing number of millennials in the workplace will support this shift, as they are more accustomed to instantaneous information. This will in turn lead to a rise of mobile apps, social collaboration, and messaging to replace the standard email.[194]

Mobile Technologies

Use of mobile technologies will only grow and expand to other HR functions in addition to m-learning, health monitoring, mobile portals, and mobile HR applications. Mobile performance support, mobile coaching, mobile intelligent assistants, and mobile analytics will become increasingly mainstream.[195] With the growth in mobile usage, expect new laws to emerge and a raised awareness regarding organizations' reimbursement and compliance issues associated with BYOD.[196] Future HR platforms will be entirely mobile and cloud.[197]

Big Data and Analytics

Predictive analytics will take metrics to a new level (e.g., pinpointing the characteristics of best-performing employees and targeting candidates sharing those characteristics). Bersin of Deloitte tells us that data analytics will be used to harness people data and predictive analytics will provide deeper insights for HR to understand the workforce and predict future trends.[198] Nevertheless, even though data analytics and predictive analytics are becoming increasingly more advanced, there will still be a need for human discernment to interpret and react to the results.

Cloud Computing and Security

Bartoletti et al. indicate that with the cloud applications there will still be a concern about security. True security remains in your own hands. Therefore, "bring your own encryption" (encryption by the organization and not the cloud service provider) will be the answer cloud providers offer to HR departments and organizations.[199]

MOOCs and Corporate Learning

MOOCs providing free Internet learning and learning experiences will become increasingly more attractive to organizations. This is largely because millennials (soon to be the largest demographic in the workplace) have indicated that the ability to learn on the job is incentive to stay. Thus, organizations will shift from traditional instruction to coaching, apprenticeship, expert support, and learning that is video-based, with cognitive learning tools that push learning at the right time.[200] The role of HR will expand further to identify and develop these opportunities.

IoT

HR professionals and managers will shift from individual performance evaluation to rely on aggregated performance data gathered using IoT to sense how the team is doing. Data analyzed by task type will help individuals understand when they perform certain tasks best. IoT sensors will even communicate availability of empty desks to employees who work at temporary desks. Workers will rate the quality of a meeting and give planners immediate feedback for productive meetings by entering information into a kiosk, which will then provide insight into how to improve meetings. HR will have instantaneous feedback and will be expected to respond and adjust.[201]

AI/Robotics

Digital HR requires that employees have access to self-services, and this will be enabled by AI and robotic process automation. AI is on the rise and will become even more important in the future. For the field of HR, AI assists in performing an array of tasks from answering employee questions about topics such as benefits and timekeeping to finding appropriate developmental training opportunities and career planning.[202]

The rise of robotics has also demonstrated many ways in which administrivia can be accomplished by a robot.[203] Desplechin provides the following examples: "Using automated and intelligent filters for recruitment, using robots for interviews, or having chatbots act as human resource assistants in order to answer recurring questions from employees."[204] Before you begin hyperventilating, just remember that as repetitive jobs go away, new HR job categories and types will arise.

Blockchain

One technology trend that shows promise for HR data security is blockchain. What is it? According to Baker, "a blockchain is a distributed, shared digital ledger made up of a trail of validated facts."[205] Everyone who has access to the ledger receives the information and validates its accuracy before it is replicated, shared, and synchronized among the entities. And here is the most compelling aspect of blockchain: it is "virtually impossible to tamper with since each block of information references the block before it."[206] The security aspect alone is causing its appeal to soar; people are very excited about this technology.

What are its uses? Blockchain can be used to verify recruitment information supplied by applicants. It is also helpful to track an employee's informal learning and training. The point is that it verifies and reconciles (or not) information from multiple sources rather than the recruiter having to do that. Other applications are sure to emerge. Keep your eyes on this technology. You will hear more about it.

YOU, FUTURE HR TECHNOLOGIES, AND STRATEGIC THINKING

Strategic thinking and strategic planning are not the same thing. In the future, the ability to think strategically will be a requirement for HR professionals. The logic for this statement proceeds from the fact that HRBPs have a role as strategic partners. The demands of the position require developing an HR strategic plan as well as an HR technology plan. So it follows that, in order to contribute in this manner, we must think strategically.

Strategic thinking is defined as "a distinctive management activity whose purpose is to discover novel, imaginative strategies which can rewrite the rules of the competitive game; and to envision potential futures significantly different from the present."[207] "Strategic thinking involves the ability to be conceptual, systems–oriented, directional (linking the future with the past) and opportunistic."[208]

With the advancements in HR technologies, HR professionals need to lead the way with strategic thinking. It is time to use our conceptual skills to envision a future that connects the organization's business strategy with an HR strategy that maximizes the potential of it greatest resource: the employees. We must take responsibility, not only to plan but to consider new ways of handling the many challenges and opportunities that face HR. Armed with knowledge of the technologies that can assist in recruiting, selecting, hiring, and developing employees with the appropriate skill sets who will best fulfill the organization's priorities, we will strategize to find new ways to create the conditions where HR's strategic objectives and those of the organization as a whole can be realized. This can only be done with the proper tools selected by strategic thinkers. We can no longer sit on the sidelines and allow others to dictate how HR will conduct its business. As key business partners and important decision makers, we will create an HR plan and technology strategy that support the organization's mission and vision as well as provide forward impetus for increased efficiencies and effectiveness in the HR department.

We will develop our own strategic thinking capabilities by joining professional organizations, where we can access information about technology best practices and benchmarking. We will prepare for the future and embrace it without fear, leading the way armed with the skills to be change agents and workplace activists who develop and support the employees who are our customers.

Developing a plan in order to stay ahead of the technology curve is wise. We will conclude, then, with your personal charge regarding thinking strategically about HR technologies while looking toward the future:

- Find the best technology resources (do your due diligence).
- Collaborate with others.
- Question fearlessly.
- Learn continuously.
- Involve stakeholders in your technology decisions.
- Keep up to date on current and emerging technologies.
- Be aware of technology-related legal issues.
- Contribute to technology-related efforts.
- Join a professional association or community of practice.
- Seek the good of the organization and its employees in all of your technology decisions.
- Contribute to the intentional and informed design of your organization's HR technology strategy.
- Think strategically.

If you follow these guiding principles, you will be a leader who uses strategic thinking and positively influences the HR technology decision-making in your workplace.

Digging Deeper

Bersin, Josh. 2016. *HR Technology Disruptions for 2017: Nine Trends Reinventing the HR Software Market.* Perspective 2016. Oakland: Deloitte Development LLC.

Bughin, Jacques, Tanguy Catlin, and Laura LaBerge. 2017. *How Digital Reinventors Are Pulling Away from the Pack.* Survey, McKinsey and Company, October 2017. https://www.mckinsey. com/business-functions/digital-mckinsey/our-insights/ how-digital-reinventors-are-pulling-away-from-the-pack.

Johannessen, Jon–Arild, ed. 2016. *The Future of the HR-Department.* CreateSpace Independent Publishing.

Kotter, John P. 2012. *Leading Change.* Boston: Harvard Business Review Press.

Meister, Jeanne C., and Kevin J. Mulcahy. 2017. *The Future Workplace Experience: 10 Rules for Mastering Disruption in Recruiting and Engaging Employees.* New York: McGraw Hill Education.

Endnotes

Chapter 1. Technology and Its Impact on Human Resources and Business Professionals

1. Josh Bersin et al., "Introduction: Rewriting the Rules for the Digital Age," in *Rewriting the Rules for the Digital Age: 2017 Global Human Capital Trends*, ed. Bill Pelster and Jeff Schwartz (London: Deloitte University Press, 2017), 1–16.

2. Ed Frauenheim, "HR 2018 Future View," *Workforce Management*, December 2008, 1, 18–23, http://www.workforce.com/2008/12/19/hr-2018-future-view/.

3. Margaret Rouse, "Human Capital Management (HCM)," TechTarget, September 2017, http://searchhrsoftware.techtarget.com/definition/human-capital-management-HCM.

4. Frauenheim, "HR 2018 Future View."

5. Ian Hunter et al., *HR Business Partners*, 2nd ed. (New York: Routledge, 2016), 12–13.

6. Dave Ulrich et al., *Victory through Organization: Why the War for Talent Is Failing Your Company and What You Can Do about It* (New York: McGraw-Hill, 2017), 20–21.

7. Julie Goran, Laura LaBerge, and Ramesh Srinivasan, "Culture for a Digital Age," *McKinsey Quarterly*, July 2017, 1–13, https://www. mckinsey.com/business-functions/digital-mckinsey/our-insights/culture-for-a-digital-age.

8. Goran, LaBerge, and Srinivasan, 12–13.

9. Phillip Decker et al., "Predicting Implementation Failure in Organization Change," *Journal of Organizational Culture, Communications and Conflict* 16, no. 2 (2012): 29–49.

10. Michael R. Mabe, "Strategic Planning: 'Magic-Bullet' or Sleight of Hand," *Library Leadership and Management* 31, no. 4 (2017): 1–18.

Chapter 2. Technology Trends in Digital Human Resources

11. *Merriam-Webster*, s.v. "social networking (n.)," last updated January 30, 2018, https://www.merriam-webster.com/dictionary/social%20 networking.

12. Margaret Rouse, "Data Analytics (DA)," *TechTarget*, last updated December 2016, http://searchdatamanagement.techtarget.com/ definition/data-analytics.

13. James Bucki, "Learn about the Benefits of Mobile Computing," *Operations and Technology* (blog), *The Balance*, last updated October 15, 2017, https://www.thebalance.com/ definition-of-mobile-computing-2533640.

14. Vangie Beal, "Cloud Computing," Webopedia, 2018, https://www. webopedia.com/TERM/C/cloud_computing.html.

15. Beal.

16. Andrew Meola, "What Is the Internet of Things (IoT)?," *Business Insider*, December 19, 2016, http://www.businessinsider.com/ what-is-the-internet-of-things-definition-2016-8.

17. Dinah Wisenberg Brin, "A Web of Devices Will Reshape the Workforce," *Society for Human Resource Management*, May 2016, https://www.shrm.org/hr-today/news/hr-magazine/0516/pages/0516-internet-of-things.aspx.

18. CBInsights, "Cybersecurity's Next Frontier: 80+ Companies Using Artificial Intelligence to Secuire the Future in One Infographic," research brief, June 9, 2017, https://www.cbinsights.com/research/cybersecurity-artificial-intelligence-startups-market-map/.

19. John White, "Private vs. Public Cloud: What's the Difference?," *Expedient Blog*, 2018, https://www.expedient.com/blog/private-vs-public-cloud-whats-difference/.

20. White.

21. White.

22. Techopedia, "Community Cloud," accessed February 20, 2018, https://www.techopedia.com/definition/26559/community-cloud.

23. Mike Wheatley, "Corporate 'No-Cloud' Policies to Be Extinct by 2020, Gartner Says," *Silicon Angle*, July 5, 2016, https://siliconangle.com/blog/2016/07/05/corporate-no-cloud-policies-to-be-extinct-by-2020-gartner-says/.

24. Beal, "Cloud Computing."

25. Vangie Beal, "Private Cloud," Webopedia, 2018, https://www.webopedia.com/TERM/P/private_cloud.html.

26. Patrick Willer, "How the Internet of Things Will Impact HR," *Talent Management and HR*, May 6, 2016, https://www.tlnt.com/how-the-internet-of-things-will-impact-hr.

27. Pelster and Schwartz, *Rewriting the Rules*.

Chapter 3. Converging Trends Using Social Media as an Example

28. Lon Safko, *The Social Media Bible: Tactics, Tools and Strategies for Business Success*, 3rd ed. (Hoboken, NJ: John Wiley and Sons, 2012), 5.

29. "Moblog," Techopedia, 2018, https://www.techopedia.com/definition/2959/moblog.

30. Berger and Berger, *Talent Management Handbook*, 322–23.

31. Wikipedia, s.v. "Wiki," last modified January 19, 2018, 01:49, https://en.wikipedia.org/wiki/Wiki.

32. Lisa Guerin, *Smart Policies for Workplace Technologies: Email, Blogs, Cell Phones, and More*, 5th ed. (Berkeley: Nolo, 2017).

33. Barry Lawrence, "HR Must Mash-Up to Move Up," *HR Leads Business* (blog), HR Certification Institute, November 2, 2016, https://www.hrci.org/community/blogs-and-announcements/hr-leads-business-blog/hr-leads-business/2016/11/02/hr-must-mash-up-to-move-up.

34. Jean Paul Isson and Jesse S. Harriott, *People Analytics in the Era of Big Data: Changing the Way You Attract, Acquire, Develop, and Retain Talent* (Hoboken, NJ: John Wiley and Sons, 2016).

35. Isson and Harriott, 166.

36. Isson and Harriott, 157–67.

37. "Social Recruiting Center," *Recruiter*, 2017, https://www.recruiter.com/social-recruiting.html.

38. Willer, "Internet of Things."

39. Josh Bersin, Joe Mariani, and Kelly Monahan, "Will IoT Technology Bring Us the Quantified Employee? The Internet of Things in Human Resources," *Deloitte Insights*, May 24, 2016, https://www2.deloitte.com/insights/us/en/focus/internet-of-things/people-analytics-iot-human-resources.html.

40. Lin Grensing-Pophal, *Human Resource Essentials: Your Guide to Starting and Running the HR Function,* 2nd ed. (Alexandria: Society for Human Resource Management, 2010), 178.

Chapter 4. Technology-Enabled Learning Environments

41. Vangie Beal, "E-learning," Webopedia, 2018, https://www.webopedia.com/TERM/E/e_learning.html.

42. Shilpi Kumari, "Personalised, Flexible and Blended Learning Features of Moodle-LMS," *Educational Quest* 7, no. 1: 53–56.

43. Edward Hess, *Learn or Die: Using Science to Build a Leading Edge Learning Organization* (New York: Columbia Business School Publishing, 2014), 46.

44. Josh Bersin, "Employee Learning Enters the Digital Age: It's Time to Give Employees Access to Content When and Where They Want It," *HR Magazine* 62, no. 6 (2017): 59–60.

45. See the website: http://voicethread.psu.edu/.

46. Tony Bingham and Marcia Conner, *The New Social Learning: Connect. Collaborate. Work*, 2nd ed. (Alexandria: ATD Press, 2015), 8.

47. YouTube, "YouTube for Press," last accessed February 20, 2018, https://www.youtube.com/yt/about/press/.

48. Christine Comaford, "Four 2017 Topics that Bad Leaders Will Ignore and Great Leaders Will Embrace," *Leadership* (blog), *Forbes*, December 31, 2016, https://www.forbes.com/sites/christinecomaford/2016/12/31/four-2017-topics-that-bad-leaders-will-ignore-great-leaders-will-embrace/#25e0c0371047.

49. Laura Wood, "Gamification in the E-learning Marketplace—2015 Study," *PR Newswire*, April 10, 2015, https://www.prnewswire.com/news-releases/gamification-in-the-e-learning-marketplace---2015-study-499366101.html.

50. Lisa A. Giacumo and Jeroen Breman, "Emerging Evidence on the Use of Big Data and Analytics in Workplace Learning: A Systematic Literature Review," *Quarterly Review of Distance Education* 17, no. 4 (2016): 21–38.

Chapter 5. Learning-Technology Selection

51. John P. Kotter, *Leading Change* (Boston: Harvard Business Publishing, 2012).

52. Tanya Elias, "71. Universal Instructional Design Principles for Mobile Learning," *International Review of Research in Open Distributed Learning* 12, no. 2 (2011): 1–7.

53. Bob Little, "The Purchasing – and Practical Benefits – of a Learning Management System," *Industrial and Commercial Training* 47, no 7 (2015): 382.

Chapter 6. Mobile Learning

54. Ulrich et al., *Victory through Organization*, 20.

55. Cait Etherington, "Mobile Learning around the World," *eLearning Inside News*, January 28, 2017, https://news.elearninginside.com/mobile-learning-around-world/.

56. "Mobile Phone User Penetration as Percentage of the Population Worldwide from 2013 to 2019," *Statista*, 2018, https://www.statista.com/statistics/470018/mobile-phone-user-penetration-worldwide/

57. Elias, "Universal Instructional Design."

58. Elias.

59. Statista, "Number of Mobile Phone Users Worldwide from 2013 to 2019 (in Billions)," 2018, https://www.statista.com/statistics/274774/forecast-of-mobile-phone-users-worldwide/.

60. *Cambridge Advanced Learner's Dictionary*, s.v. "vodcast (n.)," accessed January 24, 2018, https://dictionary.cambridge.org/us/dictionary/english/vodcast.

61. *Cambridge Academic Content Dictionary*, s.v. "virtual reality (n.)," accessed January 24, 2018, https://dictionary.cambridge.org/us/dictionary/english/virtual-reality.

62. Sagar Chavan, "Augmented Reality vs. Virtual Reality: Differences and Similarities," *International Journal of Advanced Research in Computer Engineering and Technology* (hereafter IJARCET) 5, no. 6 (2016): 1947–52.

63. Chavan, 1947.

64. Boris Dzhingarov, "Mobile Technology Can Promote Productivity and Profitability," *Monetary Library* (blog), Biz Community, September 1, 2017, http://www.bizcommunity.com/PressOffice/PressRelease.aspx?i=207623&ai=166884.

65. Dave Chaffey, "Mobile Marketing Statistics Compilation," *Smart Insights* Blog, January 30, 2018, https://www.smartinsights.com/mobile-marketing/mobile-marketing-analytics/mobile-marketing-statistics/.

66. Catrin Cooper, "5 Ways Mobile Technology Boosts Workplace Productivity," *Productivity* (blog), HR C-Suite, October 5, 2017, http://hrcsuite.com/mobile-technology/.

67. See the Microsoft web page: https://support.office.com/en-us/article/Use-a-mobile-device-to-work-with-SharePoint-Online-sites-a99f2acf-381a-442c-b305-3e74c251bcb6?ui=en-US&rs=en-US&ad=US.

68. Robert L. Brady, Mobile Learning: What You Need to Know (Brentwood, TN: Business and Legal Resources, 2015).

69. Paul Lannon and Phillip Schreiber, "BYOD Policies: Striking the Right Balance," HR Magazine 61, no. 1 (2016): 71–72.

Chapter 7. Training or Performance Support?

70. Tony O'Driscoll and Jan Cross, "In Her Own Words: Gloria Gery on Performance," Performance Improvement Journal 44, no. 8 (2005): 5.

71. Conrad Gottfredson and Bob Mosher, "Technology to the Rescue," Talent Development 69, no. 8 (2015): 46–51, https://events.td.org/Home/Publications/Magazines/TD/TD-Archive/2015/08/Technology-to-the-Rescue.

72. Raman Attri and Wing Wu, "E-learning Strategies at Workplace That Support Speed to Proficiency in Complex Skills" (presentation at the International Conference on e-Learning, Kuala Lampur, Malaysia, June 2016), 176.

73. Mason Martin, "The Many Benefits of Mobile Performance Support," Learning Solutions Magazine, January 28, 2015, https://www.learningsolutionsmag.com/articles/1612/the-many-benefits-of-mobile-performance-support.

74. O'Driscoll and Cross, "In Her Own Words," 6.

75. Ted Schadler, Josh Bernoff, and Julie Ask, The Mobile Mind Shift: Engineer Your Business to Win in the Mobile Moment (Cambridge, MA: Groundswell Press, 2014), 142.

76. Attri and Wu, "E-learning Strategies," 180.

77. Bill Gates, "The Power of the Natural User Interface," Gates Notes (blog), October 28, 2011, https://www.gatesnotes.com/About-Bill-Gates/The-Power-of-the-Natural-User-Interface.

78. Scott McCormick, "12 Types of Work-Based Performance Support Tools You Can Use Today," Float Blog, January 20, 2016, https://gowithfloat.com/2016/01/12-types-of-work-based-performance-support-tools-get-started-today/.

79. Scott McCormick and Gary Woodill, The Rise of Work-Based Performance Support Systems in the Digital Age, white paper (Float, 2015), 10, https://gowithfloat.com/wp-content/uploads/2016/01/

Rise-of-Work-Based-Performance-Support-Systems-White-
Paper.pdf.

80. Magpi, "Magpi Mobile App Brings Green Data Collection and
Communication to Groundwork Denver," June 6, 2015, https://
home.magpi.com/magpi-mobile-app-brings-green-data-collection-
and-communication-to-groundwork-denver/.

81. Magpi.

82. Magpi.

Chapter 8. Handling HR Talent Management Functions

83. Berger and Berger, *Talent Management Handbook*.

84. Michael J. Kavanagh, Mohan Thite, and Richard D. Johnson, *Human
Resource Information Systems: Basics, Applications, and Future Directions*,
3rd ed. (Thousand Oaks, CA: Sage Publishing, 2015), 70.

85. Wikipedia, s.v. "Single source of truth," last modified November 13,
2017, 22:03, https://en.wikipedia.org/wiki/Single_source_of_truth.

86. Wikipedia, s.v. "Single version of the truth," last modified
August 7, 2017, 09:18, https://en.wikipedia.org/wiki/
Single_version_of_the_truth.

87. Kavanagh, Thite, and Johnson, *Human Resource Information Systems*, 70.

88. Margaret Rouse, "Data Scrubbing (Data Cleansing)," *TechTarget*,
August 2010, http://searchdatamanagement.techtarget.com/
definition/data-scrubbing.

89. Isson and Harriott, *People Analytics*, 6.

90. Josh Bersin, "10 Things We Know about People Analytics,"
CIO Journal, December 3, 2015, http://deloitte.wsj.com/
cio/2015/12//03/10-things-we-know-about-people-analytics.

91. Isson and Herriott, *People Analytics*, 2–32.

92. "Scorecard: How Can the Balanced Scorecard Be Applied to Human Resources?," HR Q&As, Society for Human Resource Management, March 17, 2015, https://www.shrm. org/resourcesandtools/tools-and-samples/hr-qa/pages/ howcanthebalancedscorecardbeappliedtohumanresources.aspx.

93. Sarah Dobson, "HR Metrics Not Regularly Used by Finance Departments: Survey," *Canadian HR Reporter* 28, no. 17 (2015): 21.

94. Jac Fitz-Enz and John R. Mattox II, *Predictive Analytics for Human Resources* (Hoboken, NJ: Wiley, 2014), 90–93.

95. Fitz-Enz and Mattox, 92–93.

96. Margaret Rouse, "Business Intelligence Dashboard," *TechTarget*, last updated November 2010, http://searchbusinessanalytics.techtarget. com/definition/business-intelligence-dashboard.

97. Harold Kerzner, *Project Management Metrics, KPIs, and Dashboards: A Guide to Measuring and Monitoring Project Performance*, 2nd ed. (New York: Wiley, 2013), 254–55.

98. Kavanagh, Thite, and Johnson, *Human Resource Information Systems*, 471–75.

99. Kavanagh, Thite, and Johnson, 316.

Chapter 9. Information Systems Designed for Human Resources

100. Kavanagh, Thite, and Johnson, *Human Resource Information Systems*, 19–20.

101. Hunter et al., *HR Business Partners*.

102. Kavanagh, Thite, and Johnson, *Human Resource Information Systems*, 16.

103. Kavanagh, Thite, and Johnson, 16.

104. Ulrich et al., *Victory through Organization*, 55.

105. Kavanagh, Thite, and Johnson, *Human Resource Information Systems*, 17.

106. Hunter et al., *HR Business Partners*, 12.

107. Hunter et al., 37.

108. Brent Dykes, "Single Version of Truth: Why Your Company Must Speak the Same Data Language," *Forbes*, January 10, 2018, https://www.forbes.com/sites/brentdykes/2018/01/10/single-version-of-truth-why-your-company-must-speak-the-same-data-language/.

109. Josh Bersin, "Transformative Tech A Disruptive Year Ahead," *HR Magazine* 62, no. 1 (2017): 28.

110. Jennifer Arnold, "A Sounder Selection Process," *HR Magazine* 62, no. 8 (2017): 36–40.

111. Anand Swaminathan, "Harnessing Scale to Drive Successful Digital Transformations," *Digital McKinsey*, August 2017, https://www.mckinsey.com/business-functions/digital-mckinsey/our-insights/harnessing-scale-to-drive-successful-digital-transformations.

Chapter 10. E-recruiting

112. Ulrich et al., *Victory through Organization*.

113. Jen Schramm, "The Internet of Things," *HR Magazine* 59, no. 10 (2014): 57.

114. Michael Lawson, "Shifting to a Next Generation Workplace," *Public Management* 99, no. 1 (2017): 18.

115. Andy Headworth, *Social Media Recruitment: How to Successfully Integrate Social Media into Recruitment Strategy* (Philadelphia: Kogan Page, 2015).

116. Headworth, 102.

117. Margaret Rouse, "Applicant Tracking System (ATS)," *TechTarget*, last updated November 2010, http://searchcio.techtarget.com/definition/applicant-tracking-system.

118. Dave Zielinski, "7 Reasons to Love Your ATS," *HR Magazine* 60, no. 8 (2015): 30–34.

119. A. Jonathan Trafimow, "The Legal ABCs of E-recruiting," *Workforce*, March 20, 2014, http://www.workforce.com/2014/03/20/the-legal-abcs-of-e-recruiting/.

120. Office of Federal Contract Compliance Programs, "Internet Applicant Recordkeeping Rule," accessed February 20, 2018, https://www.dol.gov/ofccp/regs/compliance/faqs/iappfaqs.htm#Q1GI.

Chapter 11. The Powerful Human Resource Portal

121. Kavanagh, Thite, and Johnson, Human Resource Information, 463.

122. Eugene Valeriano and Marlon Gamido, HRIS, IPMIS and PS: An Integrated System with Employee Portal (Saarbrücken, Deu.: Lambert Academic Publishing, 2016), 10.

123. Karen Thoreson and Nijah Fudge, "Attracting Talent: Research Recommends Steps to Take," *Public Management*, March 2016, 26.

Chapter 12. Managing Knowledge

124. Philip Robert Harris, *Managing the Knowledge Culture: A Guide for Human Resource Professionals and Managers in the 21st Century Workplace* (Amherst: HRD Press Inc., 2005).

125. E. Wenger, Richard McDermott, and William M. Snyder, *Cultivating Communities of Practice* (Boston: Harvard Business School Press, 2002).

126. Stephanie Barnes and Nick Milton, *Designing a Successful KM Strategy: A Guide for the Knowledge Management Professional* (Medford, NJ: Information Today Inc., 2016).

127. Sandra Haimila, "Trend-Setting Products of 2017," *KM World*, September 14, 2017, http://www.kmworld.com/Articles/Editorial/Features/KMWorld-Trend-Setting-Products-of-2017-120392.aspx.

128. Kevin Linderman, Roger Schroeder, and Janine Sanders, "A Knowledge Framework Underlying Process Management," *Decision Sciences Journal* 41, no. 4 (2010): 702.

129. Silvia Martelo-Landroguez and David Martin-Ruiz, "Managing Knowledge to Create Customer Service Value," *Journal of Service Theory and Practice* 26, no. 4 (2015): 473–75.

130. Sales Force, "What Is CRM?," accessed February 21, 2018, https://www.salesforce.com/form/sem/sales_salesforce-b.jsp.

131. Barnes and Milton, *Successful KM Strategy*, 107.

Chapter 13. Groupware for Collaboration

132. Margaret Rouse, "Groupware," *TechTarget*, last modified September 2005, http://searchdomino.techtarget.com/definition/groupware.

133. Deborah Waddill and Michael Marquardt, "Adult Learning Theories and the Practice of Action Learning," in *Action Learning in Practice*, ed. Michael Pedler (London: Gower, 2011).

134. Elizabeth Agnvall, "Meetings Go Virtual," *HR Magazine* 54, no. 1 (2009): 74.

135. Margaret R. Lee, *Leading Virtual Project Teams: Adapting Leadership Theories and Communications Techniques to 21st Century Organizations,* Best Practices and Advances in Program Management Series (Boca Raton: CRC Press, 2014), 2.

136. Sandra Morley, Kathryn Cormican, and Paul Folan, "An Analysis of Virtual Team Characteristics: A Model for Virtual Project Managers," *Journal of Technology Management and Innovation* 10, no. 1 (2015): 1–15.

137. Lee Michael Katz, "The Case for Face Time," *HR Magazine* 60, no. 7 (2015): 70.

138. K. Swan and P. Shea, "The Development of Virtual Learning Communities," in *Learning Together Online: Research on Asynchronous*

Learning Networks, ed. Starr Roxanne Hiltz and Ricki Goldman (Mahwah, NJ: Lawrence Erlbaum Associates Publishers, 2005), 243.

Chapter 14. Technology-Enabled Evaluation and Feedback

139. Darlene Russ-Eft and Hallie Preskill, *Evaluation in Organizations* (New York: Basic Books, 2009), 4.

140. Russ-Eft and Preskill, 11–15.

141. Russ-Eft and Preskill, 209–28.

142. Fitz-Enz and Mattox, *Predictive Analytics,* 4.

143. Techopedia, "Unstructured Data," accessed February 21, 2018, https://www.techopedia.com/definition/13865/unstructured-data.

144. Timothy King, "Key Differences between Structured and Unstructured Data," *Data Management Solutions Review, Best Practices,* July 25, 2017, https://solutionsreview.com/data-management/key-differences-between-structured-and-unstructured-data/.

145. King.

146. Techopedia, "Data Lake," accessed February 21, 2018, https://www.techopedia.com/definition/30172/data-lake.

147. Boris Ewenstein, Bryan Hancock, and Asmus Komm, "Ahead of the Curve: The Future of Performance Management," *McKinsey Quarterly,* May 2016, https://www.mckinsey.com/business-functions/organization/our-insights/ahead-of-the-curve-the-future-of-performance-management.

148. Ewenstein, Hancock and Komm.

149. Pelster and Schwartz, *Rewriting the Rules.*

150. Milligan, "HR Then and Now."

151. ClearCompany, "An Essential Checklist for Getting Your HR Department Back in Order," accessed January 29, 2018, http://info.

clearcompany.com/hubfs/ClearCompany-An-Essential-Checklist-for-Getting-Your-HR-Department-Back-in-Order.

152. Nina Mehta, "Flexible Performance," *Training Journal* 7 (2016): 24.

153. Mehta, 25.

154. Nathan Sloan et al., "Performance Management: Playing a Winning Hand; 2017 Global Capital Trends," *Deloitte Insights*, February 28, 2017, https://www2.deloitte.com/insights/us/en/focus/human-capital-trends/2017/redesigning-performance-management.html.

155. Sloan et al.

156. Sequoia Star et al., "Performance Measurement and Performance Indicators: A Literature Review and a Proposed Model for Practical Adoption," *Human Resource Development Review* 15, no. 2 (2016): 158.

157. Kavanagh, Thite, and Johnson, *Human Resource Information Systems*, 461–68.

158. Jenna Gilligan, "TalentFirst Rebrands as iCoachFirst," *Business Wire*, June 5, 2017, https://www.businesswire.com/news/home/20170605005607/en/TalentFirst-Rebrands-iCoachFirst.

159. Paula Bernier, "Human Capital Management," *Customer* 33, no. 6 (2015): 20.

160. Association for Talent Development Staff, "Building Talent: The Very Best of 2017," *Talent Development* 71, no. 10 (2017), https://www.td.org/magazines/td-magazine/building-talent-the-very-best-of-2017.

161. Vijay Bankar, "Talent Management Needs Help: Change the Way You Manage People," *Excellence Essentials*, October 21, 2016, https://www.hr.com/en/magazines/all_articles/talent-management-needs-help-change-the-way-you-ma_iujjr69c.html.

162. Pelster and Schwartz, *Rewriting the Rules*, 68.

163. Don Dillman, Jolene D. Smyth, and Leah Melani Christian, *Mail and Internet Surveys: The Tailored Design Method*, 4th ed. (New York: John Wiley and Sons Inc., 2014), 16–17.

164. See the website: https://www.fedview.opm.gov/.

Chapter 15. Social Networks

165. Bingham and Conner, *New Social Learning*, 33.

166. Bingham and Conner, 19.

167. Kavanagh, Thite, and Johnson, *Human Resource Information Systems*, 568.

168. Mark Feffer, "New Connections," *HR Magazine* 60, no. 3 (2015): 46.

169. Isson and Herriott, *People Analytics*, 162.

170. Isson and Herriott, 163.

171. Kelly O. Scott and Patrick A. Fraioli Jr., "The Increasing Risks of Background Checks," *HR Magazine* 61, no. 10 (2017): 66–67.

172. Mary-Ann Russon, "Unilever Threatens to Pull Ads from Facebook and Google," BBC News, February 12, 2018, http://www.bbc.com/news/business-43032241.

173. Hallie Detrick, "Unilever Threatens to Pull Ads from Facebook and Google if They Don't Help Clean Up the Internet," *Fortune*, February 12, 2018, http://fortune.com/2018/02/12/unilever-pull-ads-facebook-google/.

174. Walter J. Andrews and Michael S. Levine, "Top 10 Employment Liability Concerns," *HR Magazine* 60, no. 6 (2015): 63–64.

Chapter 16. HR as a Strategic Partner

175. Hunter et al., *HR Business Partners*, 134–35.

176. Hunter et al., 22–25.

177. Barielle Wirth and Gary Gansle, "Jump toward Emotional Intelligence," *HR Magazine* 57, no. 10 (2012): 87.

178. Kotter, *Leading Change*, 37–153.

179. Dessler and Varkkey, *Human Resource Management*, 292.

180. Peter Northouse, *Leadership Theory and Practice*, 7th ed. (Thousand Oaks, CA: Sage Publishing, 2016), 233–35.

Chapter 17. Future Trends for Technology and HR

181. Jon-Arild Johannessen, *The Future of the HR-Department* (CreateSpace Independent Publishing, 2017); and Meister and Mulcahy, *Future Workplace Experience*, 212.

182. Meister and Mulcahy, *Future Workplace Experience*, 212.

183. Northouse, *Leadership Theory and Practice*, 366.

184. Josh Bersin, *HR Technology Disruptions for 2017: Nine Trends Reinventing the HR Software Market, Perspective 2016* (Oakland, CA: Deloitte Development LLC, 20156), 15.

185. Milligan, "HR Then and Now," 38.

186. Meister and Mulcahy, *Future Workplace Experience*, 212.

187. Meister and Mulcahy, 215.

188. Milligan, "HR Then and Now," 40.

189. Meister and Mulcahy, *Future Workplace Experience*, 212.

190. CBS News, "Job Ads on Facebook Raise Concerns about Age Discrimination, Report Says," *MoneyWatch*, December 20, 2017, https://www.cbsnews.com/news/facebook-job-ads-age-discrimination-report/.

191. Meister and Mulcahy, *Future Workplace Experience*, 206–7.

192. Hunter et al., *HR Business Partners*, 45–49.

193. Aliah D. Wright, "Study: Employers' Failure to Adopt Tech Trends May Damage Engagement," Society for Human Resource Management, June 30, 2015, https://www.shrm.org/ResourcesAndTools/ hr-topics/technology/Pages/How-Ignoring-Tech-Trends-Can- Damage-Employee-Engagement.aspx.

194. Wright.

195. Meister and Mulcahy, *Future Workplace Experience*, 21, 58, 90, 96–98.

196. Paul Lannon and Phillip Schreiber, "BYOD Policies: Striking the Right Balance." *HR Magazine* 61, no. 1 (2016): 71–72.

197. Bersin, *HR Technology Disruptions*, 18.

198. Bersin, 20.

199. Dave Bartoletti et al., *Predictions 2017: Customer-Obsessed Enterprises Launch Cloud's Second Decade* (Cambridge, MA: Forrester, 2016), 8.

200. Meister and Mulcahy, *Future Workplace Experience*, 63–66.

201. Bersin, *HR Technology Disruptions*, 8.

202. Conner Forrest, "IBM Watson: What Are Companies Using It For?," *AI and the Future of Business* (ZDNet special feature), September 1, 2015, http://www.zdnet.com/article/ ibm-watson-what-are-companies-using-it-for.

203. Martin Ford, *Rise of the Robots: Technology and the Threat of a Jobless Future* (New York: Basic Books, 2015), 86–88.

204. Agnes Desplechin, "Robots Are Moving into Our Human Resources Functions," *Digitalist Magazine*, September 21, 2017, http://www.digitalistmag.com/future-of-work/2017/09/21/ robots-moving-into-human-resources-functions-05380377.

205. Pam Baker, 2018. "Why Blockchain for Recruitment Might Be a Future HR Trend," *TechTarget Essential Guide*, February

2017, http://searchhrsoftware.techtarget.com/feature/
Why-blockchain-for-recruitment-might-be-a-future-HR-trend.

206. Baker.

207. Loizos Heracleous, "Strategic Thinking or Strategic Planning?," *Long Range Planning* 31, no. 3 (1998): 485.

208. Ellen Goldman, "Strategic Thinking at the Top," *MIT Sloan Management Review* 48, no. 4 (2007): 76.

Bibliography

Agnvall, Elizabeth. 2009. "Meetings Go Virtual." *HR Magazine* 54 (1): 74–77.

Andrews, Walter J., and Michael S. Levine. 2015. "Top 10 Employment Liability Concerns." *HRMagazine* 60, no. 6 (Jul): 63–64.

Arnold, Jennifer. 2017. "A Sounder Selection Process." *HR Magazine* 62 (8): 36–40.

Attri, Raman, and Wing Wu. 2016. "E-learning Strategies at Workplace That Support Speed to Proficiency in Complex Skills." Presentation at the International Conference on E-learning, Kuala Lampur, Malaysia, June 2016.

Baker, Pam. 2018. "HR Tech Trends: Blockchain & Mobile: How They're Reinventing Today's Talent Management Strategies." (e-guide) *TechTarget*, Last modified 2017, accessed February 13, 2018: 1–15.

Bankar, Vijay. 2016. "Talent Management Needs HELP: Change the Way You Manage People." *Talent Management Excellence Essentials:* 1–10.

Barnes, Stephanie, and Nick Milton. 2016. *Designing a Successful KM Strategy: A Guide for the Knowledge Management Professional.* Medford, NJ: Information Today.

Bartoletti, Dave, Lauren Nelson, Andras Cser, Sophia Vargas, William Martorelli, Liz Herbert, Andre Kindness, Paul Miller, Charlie Dai, and Frank Liu. 2016. *Predictions 2017: Customer-Obsessed Enterprises Launch Cloud's Second Decade.* Cambridge, MA: Forrester: 1–12.

Beal, Vangie. 2018. "Cloud Computing." Webopedia. https://www. webopedia.com/TERM/C/cloud_computing.html.

———. 2018. "E-learning." Webopedia. https://www.webopedia.com/ TERM/E/e_learning.html.

———. 2018. "Private Cloud." Webopedia. https://www.webopedia. com/TERM/P/private_cloud.html.

Berger, Lance A., and Dorothy R. Berger. 2017. *The Talent Management Handbook: Making Culture a Competitive Advantage by Acquiring, Identifying, Developing, and Promoting the Best People.* 3rd ed. New York: McGraw Hill.

Bersin, Josh. 2015. "10 Things We Know about People Analytics." *CIO Journal*, December 3, 2015. http://deloitte.wsj.com/ cio/2015/12//03/10-things-we-know-about-people-analytics.

———. 2016. *HR Technology Disruptions for 2017: Nine Trends Reinventing the HR Software Market.* Perspective 2016. Oakland: Deloitte Development LLC.

———. 2017. "Employee Learning Enters the Digital Age: It's Time to Give Employees Access to Content When and Where They Want It." *HR Magazine* 62 (6): 59–60.

———. 2017. "Transformative Tech: A Disruptive Year Ahead." *HR Magazine* 62 (1): 28–29, 31, 33–34, 36.

Bersin, Josh, Joe Mariani, and Kelly Monahan. 2016. "Will IoT Technology Bring Us the Quantified Employee? The Internet of Things in Human Resources." *Deloitte Insights*, May 24, 2016. https://www2.deloitte. com/insights/us/en/focus/internet-of-things/people-analytics-iot-human-resources.html.

Bersin, Josh, Bill Pelster, Jeff Schwartz, and Bernard van der Vyver. 2017. "Introduction: Rewriting the Rules for the Digital Age," in *Rewriting the Rules for the Digital Age: 2017 Global Human Capital Trends*, ed. Bill Pelster and Jeff Schwartz, 1–16. N.p.: Deloitte University Press.

Bingham, Tony, and Marcia Conner. 2015. *The New Social Learning: Connect. Collaborate. Work.* 2nd ed. Alexandria: ATD Press.

Brady, Robert L. 2015. *Mobile Learning: What You Need to Know.* Brentwood, TN: Business and Legal Resources.

Brin, Dinah Wisenberg. 2016. "A Web of Devices Will Reshape the Workforce." *SHRM.org*, May 01, 2016. https://www.shrm.org/hr-today/news/hr-magazine/0516/pages/0516-internet-of-things.aspx.

Bucki, James. 2017. "Learn about the Benefits of Mobile Computing." *Operations and Technology* (blog), *The Balance*, last updated October 15, 2017. https://www.thebalance.com/definition-of-mobile-computing-2533640.

Bughin, Jacques, Tanguy Catlin, and Laura LaBerge. 2017. *How Digital Reinventors Are Pulling Away from the Pack.* Survey, McKinsey and Company, October 2017. https://www.mckinsey.com/business-functions/digital-mckinsey/our-insights/how-digital-reinventors-are-pulling-away-from-the-pack.

CBInsights. 2017. "Cybersecurity's Next Fronntier: 80+ Companies Using Artificial Intelligence to Secuire the Future in One Infographic." (research brief) *CBInsights.com*, Last modified June 09, 2017, accessed February 6, 2018. https://www.cbinsights.com/research/cybersecurity-artificial-intelligence-startups-market-map/.

CBS News. 2017. "Job ads on Facebook Raise Concerns about Age Discrimination, Report Says." Money Watch. New York: CBS News., December 20, 2017. https://www.cbsnews.com/news/facebook-job-ads-age-discrimination-report/.

Chaffey, Dave. 2018. "Mobile Marketing Statistics Compilation." *Smart Insights,* January 30, 2018. https://www.smartinsights. com/mobile-marketing/mobile-marketing-analytics/ mobile-marketing-statistics/.

Chavan, Sagar. 2016. "Augmented Reality vs. Virtual Reality: Differences and Similarities." *International Journal of Advanced Research in Computer Engineering and Technology* 5 (6): 1947–52.

ClearCompany. 2018. "An Essential Checklist for Getting Your HR Department Back in Order." Accessed January 29, 2018. http://info. clearcompany.com/hubfs/ClearCompany-An-Essential-Checklist- for-Getting-Your-HR-Department-Back-in-Order.

Comaford, Christine. 2016. "Four 2017 Topics that Bad Leaders Will Ignore and Great Leaders Will Embrace." *Leadership* (blog), *Forbes,* December 31, 2016. https://www.forbes.com/sites/ christinecomaford/2016/12/31/four-2017-topics-that-bad-leaders- will-ignore-great-leaders-will-embrace/#25e0c0371047.

Cooper, Catrin. 2017. "5 Ways Mobile Technology Boosts Workplace Productivity." *Productivity* (blog), *HR C-Suite,* October 5, 2017. http:// hrcsuite.com/mobile-technology.

Davenport, Thomas H., Jeanne Harris, and Jeremy Shapiro. 2010. "Competing on Talent Analytics." *Harvard Business Review* 88 (10): 52–58.

Decker, Phillip, Roger Durand, Clifton Mayfield, Christy McCormack, David Skinner, and Grady Perdue. 2012. "Predicting Implementation Failure in Organization Change." *Journal of Organizational Culture, Communications and Conflict* 16: 29–49.

Desplechin, Agnes. 2017. "Robots are Moving Into Our Human Resources Functions." *Digitalist Magazine,* September 24, 2017. http://www.digitalistmag.com/future-of-work/2017/09/21/ robots-moving-into-human-resources-functions-05380377.

Dessler, Gary, and Biju Varkkey. 2016. *Human Resource Management*. 14th ed. Noida, IN: Pearson.

Detrick, Hallie. 2018. "Unilever Threatens to Pull Ads from Facebook and Google if They Don't Help Clean Up the Internet." *Fortune*, February 12, 2018. http://fortune.com/2018/02/12/unilever-pull-ads-facebook-google/.

Dillman, Don, Jolene D. Smyth, and Leah Melani Christian. 2014. *Mail and Internet Surveys: The Tailored Design Method*. 4th ed. New York, New York: John Wiley & Sons, Inc.

Dobson, Sarah. 2015. "HR Metrics Not Regularly Used by Finance Departments: Survey." *Canadian HR Reporter* 28 (17): 21.

Douglas, Genevieve. 2016. "HR Increasingly Adopting Cloud Technology." *Bloomberg News*, July 29, 2016. https://www.bna.com/hr-increasingly-adopting-n73014445636.

Dykes, Brent. 2018. "Single Version of Truth: Why Your Company Must Speak the Same Data Language." *Forbes*, January 10, 2018. https://www.forbes.com/sites/brentdykes/2018/01/10/single-version-of-truth-why-your-company-must-speak-the-same-data-language.

Dzhingarov, Boris. 2017. "Mobile Technology Can Promote Productivity and Profitability." *Monetary Library* (blog), Biz Community, September 01, 2017. http://www.bizcommunity.com/PressOffice/PressRelease.aspx?i=207623&ai=166884.

Elias, Tanya. 2011. "71. Universal Instructional Design Principles for Mobile Learning." *International Review of Research in Open Distributed Learning* 12 (2): 1–7.

Etherington, Cait. 2017. "Mobile Learning Around the World." *eLearning Inside News*, January 28, 2017. https://news.elearninginside.com/mobile-learning-around-world.

Ewenstein, Boris, Bryan Hancock, and Asmus Komm. 2016. "Ahead of the Curve: The Future of Performance Management." *McKinsey Quarterly*, May 2016. https://www.mckinsey. com/business-functions/organization/our-insights/ ahead-of-the-curve-the-future-of-performance-management.

Feffer, Mark. 2015. "New Connections." *HR Magazine* 60 (3): 46–50, 52.

Fernandez, Dominique Bonet, and Nabila Jawadi. 2015. "Virtual R&D Project Teams: From E-leadership to Performance." *Journal of Applied Business Research* 31 (5): 195–97.

Fitz-Enz, Jac, and John R. Mattox II. 2014. *Predictive Analytics for Human Resources*. Hoboken, NJ: Wiley.

Ford, Martin. 2015. *Rise of the Robots: Technology and the Threat of a Jobless Future*. New York: Basic Books.

Forni, Amy Ann, and Rob van der Meulen. 2016. *Gartner Says by 2020, a Corporate 'No-Cloud' Policy Will Be as Rare as a 'No-Internet' Policy Is Today: Hybrid will Be the Most Common Use of the Cloud.* (press release) Stamford, Connecticut: Gartner, June 22, 2016. https://www.gartner. com/newsroom/id/3354117.

Forrest, Conner. 2015. "IBM Watson: What Are Companies Using It For?" AI and the Future of Business, *ZDNet*, September 01, 2015. http://www.zdnet.com/article/ ibm-watson-what-are-companies-using-it-for.

Frauenheim, Ed. 2008. "HR 2018 Future View." *Workforce Management*, December 19, 2008. http://www.workforce.com/2008/12/19/ hr-2018-future-view.

Gates, Bill. 2011. "The Power of the Natural User Interface." *Gates Notes* (blog), October 28, 2011. https://www.gatesnotes.com/ About-Bill-Gates/The-Power-of-the-Natural-User-Interface.

Giacumo, Lisa A., and Jeroen Breman. 2016. "Emerging Evidence on the Use of Big Data and Analytics in Workplace Learning: A Systematic Literature Review." *Quarterly Review of Distance Education* 17 (4): 21–38.

Gilligan, Jenna. 2017. "TalentFirst Rebrands as iCoachFirst." *Business Wire*, June 05, 2017. http://www.businesswire.com/news/home/20170605005607/en/.

Goldman, Ellen. 2007. "Strategic Thinking at the Top." *MIT Sloan Management Review* 48 (4):75–81.

Goran, Julie, Laura LaBerge, and Ramesh Srinivasan. 2017. "Culture for a Digital Age." *McKinsey Quarterly*, July 2017: 1–13. https://www.mckinsey.com/business-functions/digital-mckinsey/our-insights/culture-for-a-digital-age.

Gottfredson, Conrad, and Bob Mosher. 2015. "Technology to the Rescue." *Association for Talent Development*, August 08, 2015. https://events.td.org/Home/Publications/Magazines/TD/TD-Archive/2015/08/Technology-to-the-Rescue.

Grensing-Pophal, Lin. 2010. *Human Resource Essentials: Your Guide to Starting and Running the HR Function.* 2nd ed. Alexandria: Society for Human Resource Management.

Guerin, Lisa. 2009. *Smart Policies for Workplace Technologies: Email, Blogs, Cell Phones, and More.* Berkeley: Nolo.

Haimila, Sandra. 2017. "Trend-Setting Products of 2017." *KM World*, September 14, 2017. http://www.kmworld.com/Articles/Editorial/Features/KMWorld-Trend-Setting-Products-of-2017-120392.aspx.

Harris, Philip Robert. 2005. *Managing the Knowledge Culture: A Guide for Human Resource Professionals and Managers in the 21st Century Workplace.* Amherst: HRD Press Inc.

Hashemi, Seyyed Yasser, and Parisa Sheykhi Hesarlo. 2014. "Security, Privacy and Trust Challenges in Cloud Computing and Solutions." *International Journal of Computer Network and Information Security* 8: 34–40.

Headworth, Andy. 2015. *Social Media Recruitment: How to Successfully Integrate Social Media into Recruitment Strategy*. Philadelphia: Kogan Page.

Heracleous, Loizos. 1998. "Strategic Thinking or Strategic Planning?" *Long Range Planning* 31 (3): 481–87.

Hess, Edward. 2014. *Learn or Die: Using Science to Build a Leading Edge Learning Organization*. New York: Columbia Business School Publishing.

Hunter, Ian, Jane Saunders, Allan Boroughs, and Simon Constance. 2016. *HR Business Partners*. 2nd ed. New York: Routledge.

Isson, Jean Paul, and Jesse S. Harriott. 2016. *People Analytics in the Era of Big Data: Changing the Way You Attract, Acquire, Develop, and Retain Talent*. Hoboken, NJ: John Wiley and Sons.

Johannessen, Jon-Arild, ed. 2016. *The Future of the HR-Department*. N.p.: CreateSpace Independent Publishing.

Katz, Lee Michael. 2015. "The Case for Face Time." *HR Magazine* 60 (7): 68–72.

Kavanagh, Michael J., Mohan Thite, and Richard D. Johnson. 2015. *Human Resource Information Systems: Basics, Applications, and Future Directions*. 3rd ed. Thousand Oaks, CA: Sage Publishing.

Kerzner, Harold. 2013. *Project Management Metrics, KPIs, and Dashboards: A Guide to Measuring and Monitoring Project Performance*. 2nd ed. New York: Wiley.

King, Timothy. 2018. "Structured vs. Unstructured Data. What's the Difference?" Data Management Solutions Review. Accessed

April 20, 2018. https://solutionsreview.com/data-management/ key-differences-between-structured-and-unstructured-data/.

Kotter, John P. 2012. *Leading Change*. Boston: Harvard Business Publishing.

Kumari, Shilpi. 2016. "Personaliscd, Flexible and Blended Learning Features of Moodle-LMS." *Educational Quest* 7 (1): 53–56.

Lannon, Paul, and Phillip Schreiber. 2016. "BYOD Policies: Striking the Right Balance," *HR Magazine* 61 (1): 71–72.

Lawrence, Barry. 2016. "HR Must Mash-Up to Move Up." *HR Leads Business* (blog), HR Certification Institute, November 02, 2016. https://www.hrci.org/community/blogs-and-announcements/ hr-leads-business-blog/hr-leads-business/2016/11/02/ hr-must-mash-up-to-move-up.

Lawson, Michael. 2017. "Shifting to a Next Generation Workplace." *Public Management* 99, (1): 14–18.

Lee, Margaret R. 2014. *Leading Virtual Project Teams: Adapting Leadership Theories and Communications Techniques to 21st Century Organizations*. Best Practices and Advances in Program Management Series. Boca Raton: CRC Press.

Linderman, Kevin, Roger Schroeder, and Janine Sanders. 2010. "A Knowledge Framework Underlying Process Management." *Decision Sciences Journal* 41 (4): 689–719.

Little, Bob. 2015. "The Purchasing – and Practical Benefits – of a Learning Management System." *Industrial and Commercial Training* 47 (7): 380–385.

Mabe, Michael R. 2017. "Strategic Planning: 'Magic-Bullet' or Sleight of Hand." *Library Leadership and Management* 31 (4): 1–18.

Martelo-Landroguez, Silvia, and David Martin-Ruiz. 2015. "Managing Knowledge to Create Customer Service Value." *Journal of Service Theory and Practice* 26 (4): 471–96.

Martin, Mason. 2015. "The Many Benefits of Mobile Performance Support." *Learning Solutions Magazine*, January 28, 2015. https://www.learningsolutionsmag.com/articles/1612/the-many-benefits-of-mobile-performance-support.

McCormick, Scott. 2016. "12 Types of Work-Based Performance Support Tools You Can Use Today." *Float Blog*, January 20, 2016. https://gowithfloat.com/2016/01/12-types-of-work-based-performance-support-tools-get-started-today/.

McCormick, Scott, and Gary Woodill. 2015. *The Rise of Work-Based Performance Support Systems in the Digital Age.* (white paper) Float, 2015. https://gowithfloat.com/wp-content/uploads/2016/01/Rise-of-Work-Based-Performance-Support-Systems-White-Paper.pdf.

Mehta, Nina. 2016. "Flexible Performance." *Training Journal* 7: 23–25.

Meister, Jeanne C., and Kevin J. Mulcahy. 2017. *The Future Workplace Experience: 10 Rules for Mastering Disruption in Recruiting and Engaging Employees.* New York: McGraw Hill Education.

Mercer. 2016. *The Journey to Digital HR: What Research Tells Us About Implementing a New HRIS.* (white paper) Marsh & McLennan Companies, 2016. https://www.mercer.ca/content/dam/mercer/attachments/north-america/canada/ca-2016-mercer-research-talent-hris-journey-to-digital-hr-en.pdf.

Milam-Perez, Lisa. 2017. "The Promise and Peril of 'Big Data.'" *HRMagazine* 62 (2): 72–73.

Milligan, Susan. 2017. "HR Then and Now." *HRMagazine* 62 (6): 38–41. http://www.hrmagazine-digital.com/hrmagazine/august_2017?pg=3#pg3.

Morley, Sandra, Kathryn Cormican, and Paul Folan. 2015. "An Analysis of Virtual Team Characteristics: A Model for Virtual Project Managers." *Journal of Technology Management & Innovation* 10 (1):1–15.

Northouse, Peter. 2016. *Leadership Theory and Practice*. 7th ed. Thousand Oaks, CA: Sage Publishing.

O'Driscoll, Tony, and Jan Cross. 2005. "In Her Own Words: Gloria Gery on Performance." *Performance Improvement Journal* 44 (8): 5–7.

Pelster, Bill, and Jeff Schwartz, eds. 2017. *Rewriting the Rules for the Digital Age: 2017 Deloitte Global Human Capital Trends*. N.p.: Deloitte University Press.

Recruiter.com. 2017. "Social Recruiting Center." https://www.recruiter.com/social-recruiting.html.

Rouse, Margaret. 2010. "Applicant Tracking System (ATS)." *TechTarget*, last updated November 2010. http://searchcio.techtarget.com/definition/applicant-tracking-system.

———. 2010. "Business Intelligence Dashboard." *TechTarget*, last updated November 2010. http://searchbusinessanalytics.techtarget.com/definition/business-intelligence-dashboard.

———. 2016. "Data Analytics (DA)." *TechTarget*, last updated December 2016. http://searchdatamanagement.techtarget.com/definition/data-analytics.

———. 2017. "Human Capital Management (HCM)." *TechTarget*, last updated September 2017. http://searchhrsoftware.techtarget.com/definition/human-capital-management-HCM.

Russ-Eft, Darlene, and Hallie Preskill. 2009. *Evaluation in Organizations*. New York, New York: Basic Books.

Russon, Mary-Ann. 2018. "Unilever threatens to pull ads from Facebook and Google." *BBC News*, February 12, 2018. http://www.bbc.com/news/business-43032241.

Safko, Lon. 2012. *The Social Media Bible: Tactics, Tools and Strategies for Business Success*. 3rd ed. Hoboken, NJ: John Wiley and Sons.

Schadler, Ted, Josh Bernoff, and Julie Ask. 2014. *The Mobile Mind Shift: Engineer Your Business to Win in the Mobile Moment*. Cambridge, MA: Groundswell Press.

Schawbel, Dan. 2015. "10 Workplace Trends You'll See in 2016." *Entrepreneurs* (blog), *Forbes*, November 1, 2015. https://www.forbes.com/sites/danschawbel/2015/11/01/10-workplace-trends-for-2016/#792cf894237f.

Schramm, Jen. 2014. "The Internet of Things." *HR Magazine* 59 (10): 57.

Society for Human Resource Management. 2015. "Scorecard: How Can the Balanced Scorecard Be Applied to Human Resources?" HR Q&As. March 17, 2015. https://www.shrm.org/resourcesandtools/tools-and-samples/hr-qa/pages/howcanthebalancedscorecardbeappliedtohumanresources.aspx.

Scott, Kelly O., and Patrick A. Fraioli, Jr. 2017. "The Increasing Risks of Background Checks." *HRMagazine* 61, no. 10 (Dec): 66–67.

Sequoia Star et al., 2016. "Performance Measurement and Performance Indicators: A Literature Review and a Proposed Model for Practical Adoption," *Human Resource Development Review* 15 (2): 158.

Segal, Jonathan A. 2014. "The Law and Social Media in Hiring." *HRMagazine* 59 (9): 70–72. http://proxygw.wrlc.org/login?url=https://search-proquest-com.proxygw.wrlc.org/docview/1559855356?accountid=11243.

Sloan, Nathan, Dimple Agarwal, Stacia Sherman Garr, and Karen Pastakia. 2017. *Rewriting the Rules for the Digital Age*. Deloitte University Press.

Star, Sequoia, Darlene Russ-Eft, Marc T. Braverman, and Roger Levine. 2016. "Performance Measurement and Performance Indicators: A Literature Review and a Proposed Model for Practical Adoption." *Human Resource Development Review* 15 (2): 158.

Sullivan, Dan. 2009. *Proven Portals: Best Practices for Planning, Designing, and Developing Enterprise Portals*. Boston: Pearson Education.

Statista.com. 2018. "Number of Mobile Phone Users Worldwide from 2013 to 2019 (in Billions)." Accessed February 7, 2018. https://www.statista.com/statistics/274774/forecast-of-mobile-phone-users-worldwide/.

Swan, K., and P. Shea. 2005. "The Development of Virtual Learning Communities." In *Learning Together Online: Research on Asynchronous Learning Networks*, edited by Starr Roxanne Hiltz and Ricki Goldman, 239–60. Mahwah, NJ: Lawrence Erlbaum Associates Publishers.

Swaminathan, Anand. 2017. "Harnessing Scale to Drive Successful Digital Transformations." *Digital McKinsey*, August 2017. https://www.mckinsey.com/business-functions/digital-mckinsey/our-insights/harnessing-scale-to-drive-successful-digital-transformations.

Techopedia. s.v. "Moblog." Accessed April 12, 2018. https://www.techopedia.com/definition/2959/moblog.

Thoreson, Karen, and Nijah Fudge. 2016. "Attracting Talent: Research Recommends Steps to Take." *Public Management*, March 2016: 26–27.

Trafimow, Jonathan. 2014. "The Legal ABCs of E-Recruiting." Workforce. Accessed February 8, 2018. http://www.workforce.com/2014/03/20/the-legal-abcs-of-e-recruiting/.

Ulrich, Dave, David Kryscynski, Mike Ulrich, and Wayne Brockbank. 2017. *Victory through Organization: Why the War for Talent Is Failing Your Company and What You Can Do about It*. New York: McGraw-Hill.

Valeriano, Eugene, and Marlon Gamido. 2016. *HRIS, IPMIS and PS: An Integrated System with Employee Portal*. Saarbrücken, Deu.: Lambert Academic Publishing.

Waddill, Deborah, and Michael Marquardt. 2011. "Adult Learning Theories and the Practice of Action Learning." In *Action Learning in Practice*, edited by Michael Pedler. London, U.K.: Gower.

Wenger, E., Richard McDermott, and William M. Snyder. 2002. *Cultivating Communities of Practice*. Boston, MA: Harvard Business School Press.

White, John. 2018. "Private vs. Public Cloud: What's the Difference?" *Expedient* (blog). https://www.expedient.com/blog/ private-vs-public-cloud-whats-difference.

Willer, Patrick. 2016. "How the Internet of Things Will Impact HR." Talent Management and HR, May 06, 2016. https://www.tlnt.com/ how-the-internet-of-things-will-impact-hr.

Wirth, Barielle, and Gary Gansle. 2012. "Jump toward Emotional Intelligence." *HR Magazine* 57 (10): 87–88, 90.

Wood, Laura. 2015. "Gamification in the E-learning Marketplace—2015 Study." *PR Newswire*, April 10, 2015. https://www.prnewswire.com/ news-releases/gamification-in-the-e-learning-marketplace---2015- study-499366101.html.

Wright, Aliah D. 2015. "Study: Employers' Failure to Adopt Tech Trends May Damage Engagement." Society for Human Resource Management, June 30, 2015. https://www.shrm.org/ ResourcesAndTools/hr-topics/technology/Pages/How-Ignoring- Tech-Trends-Can-Damage-Employee-Engagement.aspx.

Zielinski, Dave. 2015. "7 Reasons to Love Your ATS." *HR Magazine* 60 (8): 30–34.

Author Biography

Dr. Deborah D. Waddill, EdD, an international educator and consultant, is a professor for the Rutgers University Executive and Professional Education—Next Generation HR Program and Director of [Online] Leadership Courseware for The George Washington University's School of Medicine and Health Sciences where she is an instructor. As President of Restek Consulting, Deborah guides human resource (HR) executives, professionals and leaders around the globe—from the United States to the Netherlands, Hong Kong to the Dominican Republic, Singapore to South Africa—in their decision-making as they address the critical intersection of HR, leadership, and technology.

Dr. Waddill earned both a doctorate degree in Human Resources & Executive Leadership and an MA in Educational Technology Leadership from The George Washington University. Waddill's unique, copyrighted approach conducting Action Learning online (Action e-Learning) won the Phi Delta Kappa GWU-Chapter Dissertation Award and the Dissertation of the Year Award from the World Institute of Action Learning. She also earned the Alpha Eta Award for healthcare service and leadership as a result of her commitment to effective use of technology for leadership development.

Index

Other SHRM Titles

A Manager's Guide to Developing Competencies in HR Staff
Tips and Tools for Improving Proficiency in Your Reports
Phyllis G. Hartman, SHRM-SCP

California Employment Law: A Guide for Employers
Revised and Updated 2018 Edition
James J. McDonald, Jr., JD

Digital HR
A Guide to Technology-Enabled HR
Deborah Waddill, Ed.D.

From Hello to Goodbye: Second Edition
Proactive Tips for Maintaining Positive Employee Relations
Christine V. Walters, JD, SHRM-SCP

From We Will to At Will
A Handbook for Veteran Hiring, Transitioning, and Thriving in the Workplace
Justin Constantine with Andrew Morton

Go Beyond the Job Description
A 100-Day Action Plan for Optimizing Talents and Building Engagement
Ashley Prisant Lesko, Ph.D., SHRM-SCP

The HR Career Guide
Great Answers to Tough Career Questions
Martin Yate, CPC

HR on Purpose!!
Developing Deliberate People Passion
Steve Browne, SHRM-SCP

Mastering Consultation as an HR Practitioner
Making an Impact on Small Businesses
Jennifer Currence, SHRM-SCP

Motivation-Based Interviewing
A Revolutionary Approach to Hiring the Best
Carol Quinn

The Practical Guide to HR Analytics
Using Data to Inform, Transform, and Empower HR Decisions
Shonna D. Waters, Valerie N. Streets, Lindsay A. McFarlane, and Rachel Johnson-Murray

The Power of Stay Interviews for Engagement and Retention
Second Edition
Richard P. Finnegan

Predicting Business Success
Using Smarter Analytics to Drive Results
Scott Mondore, Hannah Spell, Matt Betts, and Shane Douthitt

The Recruiter's Handbook
A Complete Guide for Sourcing, Selecting, and Engaging the Best Talent
Sharlyn Lauby, SHRM-SCP

The SHRM Essential Guide to Employment Law
A Handbook for HR Professionals, Managers, and Businesses
Charles H. Fleischer, JD

The Talent Fix
A Leader's Guide to Recruiting Great Talent
Tim Sackett, SHRM-SCP